# BENIN

## Royal Arts of a West African Kingdom

KATHLEEN BICKFORD BERZOCK

THE ART INSTITUTE OF CHICAGO / YALE UNIVERSITY PRESS, NEW HAVEN AND LONDON

*Benin: Royal Arts of a West African Kingdom* was published in conjunction with the exhibition *Benin—Kings and Rituals: Court Arts from Nigeria*, organized by the Museum für Völkerkunde Wien – Kunsthistoriches Museum, in cooperation with the National Commission for Museums and Monuments, Nigeria, the Ethnologisches Museum – Staatliche Museen zu Berlin, the Art Institute of Chicago, and the musée du quai Branly, Paris.

Sara Lee Foundation is a Proud Corporate Sponsor.

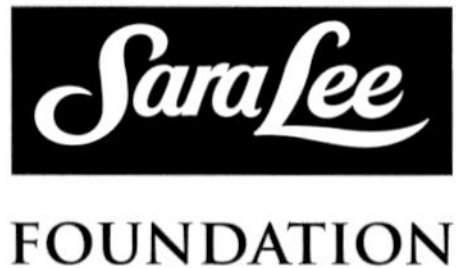

Major funding is provided by the Perucca Family Foundation.

Additional support is made possible by the Ann and Robert H. Lurie Foundation.



First edition
Library of Congress Control Number: 2008929858
ISBN: 978-0-300-13677-7

Published by
The Art Institute of Chicago
111 South Michigan Avenue
Chicago, Illinois 60603-6404
www.artic.edu

Distributed by
Yale University Press
302 Temple Street
P.O. Box 209040
New Haven, Connecticut 06520-9040
www.yalebooks.com

Produced by the Publications Department of the Art Institute of Chicago, Susan F. Rossen, Executive Director

Edited by Elizabeth Stepina, Special Projects Editor
Production by Sarah E. Guernsey, Associate Director, and Kate Kotan, Production Assistant
Photography research by Joseph Mohan, Photography Editor

Designed and typeset by Jeff Wonderland
Map prepared by Mapping Specialists, Madison, Wisconsin
Printing and binding by Classic Color, Broadview, Illinois

Front jacket: Plaque of Oba Esigie on Horseback with Attendants
(cat. 13; see p. 27)
Back jacket: Oba Erediauwa in coral regalia
(see p. 8)
Front flap: Altar Head of an Oba
(cat. 1; see p. 16)
Back flap: Hip Pendant of Iyoba Idia
(cat. 14; see p. 28)

Photography credits
Cat. 1: © Berlin, Staatliche Museen zu Berlin—Preußischer Kulturbesitz, Ethnologisches Museum (photo: Martin Franken). Cats. 2, 20: © Abuja, National Commission for Museums and Monuments Nigeria (photos: Georg Molterer). Cats. 3, 6 (top), 10, 19: © London, The Trustees of the British Museum (photos: Mike Row). Cat. 4: © Dresden, Museum für Völkerkunde Dresden, Staatliche Ethnographische Sammlungen Sachsen (SES) (photo: Eva Winkler). Cat. 5: © Leipzig, Museum für Völkerkunde zu Leipzig, Staatliche Ethnographische Sammlungen Sachsen (SES) (photo: Karin Wieckhorst). Cats. 6 (bottom), 8, 22: © Vienna, Museum für Völkerkunde Wien (photos: Alexander Rosoli). Cat. 7: © Hamburg, Museum für Kunst und Gewerbe Hamburg. Cats. 9, 15: © Edinburgh, The Trustees of the National Museums of Scotland. Cat. 11: © Antwerp, Ethnographic Museum Antwerp (photo: Hugo Maertens). Cats. 12, 17: © Berlin, Staatliche Museen zu Berlin—Preußischer Kulturbesitz, Ethnologisches Museum (photos: Dietrich Graf). Cat. 13: © Berlin, Staatliche Museen zu Berlin—Preußischer Kulturbesitz, Ethnologisches Museum (photo: Waltraud Schneider-Schütz). Cat. 14: © Seattle, Seattle Art Museum. (photo: Paul Macapia). Cat. 16: © Berlin, Staatliche Museen zu Berlin—Preußischer Kulturbesitz, Ethnologisches Museum (photo: Claudia Obrocki). Cat. 21: © Benin City, Osemwegie Ebohon (High Priest) (photo: Georg Molterer).

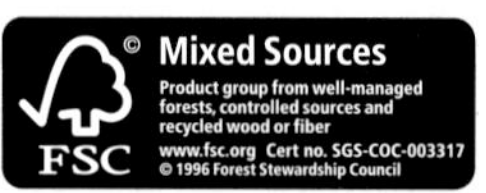

Printed on paper that contains a minimum of 30% post-consumer recovered fiber and is manufactured with renewable energy.

## ACKNOWLEDGMENTS

This book accompanies the Art Institute of Chicago's presentation of the exhibition *Benin—Kings and Rituals: Court Arts from Nigeria*, which was organized by the Museum für Völkerkunde Vienna, Kunsthistoriches Museum, with the participation of the National Commission for Museums and Monuments, Nigeria, and the Ethnologisches Museum, Staatliche Museen zu Berlin. The exhibition received the participation and support of his majesty Omo n'Oba Ukpolokpolo Erediauwa, the current oba of Benin, and I thank him especially for his contributions to the Chicago installation. The Art Institute's presentation has also benefited from the cooperation of the Chicago-based Edo Arts and Cultural Heritage Institute, and I thank Osaro Uhunmwangho, Kingsley Ehi, and Kienuwa Obaseki in particular for their friendly assistance. I am also grateful for the invaluable help we received from the staff of the Kunsthistoriches Museum Vienna, with whom the Art Institute has worked closely. This includes Director Wilfried Seipel, Christian Hölzl, and Marianne Hergovich.

Barbara Plankensteiner of the Museum für Völkerkunde Vienna deserves special recognition as the exhibition's curator and the editor of the eponymous catalogue. This small book and my presentation of the show in Chicago are derived from her initial concept. I thank her most warmly for her generosity, collegiality, and friendship over the five years that we have worked together. Additionally, I extend sincere thanks to each of the catalogue's contributors; their expertise has set a new standard in the study of Benin's art and culture. I also thank those scholars and institutions that have allowed the reproduction of their photographs in this book and in the exhibition.

Several individuals must be given special recognition for their contributions to our publication. I am particularly grateful to Cynthia and Terry Perucca, who underwrote the book and have supported the Art Institute's presentation of the exhibition and my role in it wholeheartedly. Cynthia Perucca also volunteered her time and considerable research skills to essential facets of the project beyond the scope of this book. At the Art Institute, I am also grateful to James Cuno, President and Eloise W. Martin Director, for his unflagging support. As usual, Richard F. Townsend, Chair of the Department of African and Amerindian Art, has offered intelligent advice and guidance at every turn and has willingly rolled up his sleeves to assist whenever needed. I benefit daily from his mentorship. Likewise, the staff of the Department of African and Amerindian Art—Barbara Battaglia, Elizabeth I. Pope, and Ray Ramirez—deserve my most hearty thanks for their patience and professionalism while working on this complex and demanding project and for the excellence that they bring to their jobs on a daily basis. It has been a pleasure to work once again with the outstanding staff of the Publications Department and the Department of Graphic Design, in particular editor Elizabeth Stepina and designer Jeff Wonderland. This work has also received the careful attention of Kate Kotan, Sarah Guernsey, Joseph Mohan, and Candice Wong. Additionally, the Art Institute's installation owes a great deal to a core group of professionals who have invested their time and skill to bringing it to fruition, including Markus Dohner, Erika Morris, Maria Simon, and Suzie Schnepp. Special recognition must also be given to Erin Gilbert and the Leadership Advisory Committee for their support of both the exhibition and catalogue. Countless others at the museum, too many to name in this small space, deserve my sincere thanks. I would therefore like to acknowledge the staffs of these additional departments: Design and Construction, Development, General Council, Imaging, Information Services, Marketing and Public Affairs, Museum Education, Museum Registration, Museum Shop, Objects Conservation, Physical Plant, Protection Services, and Visitors Services.

Finally, I thank the lenders to the Chicago version of the exhibition: Ethnographisches Museum Antwerp; Ethnologisches Museum, Staatliche Museen zu Berlin; the Brooklyn Museum; Rautenstrauch-Joest-Museum für Völkerkunde, Cologne; Museum für Völkerkunde Dresden, Staatliche Ethnographische Sammlungen Sachsen; National Museums of Scotland; Museum für Kunst und Gewerbe Hamburg; Museum für Völkerkunde Leipzig, Staatliche Ethnographische Sammlungen Sachsen; the British Museum; Reiss-Engelhorn-Museen Mannheim; Staatliches Museum für Völkerkunde Munich; the Metropolitan Museum of Art; National Commission for Museums and Monuments, Nigeria; Omo n'Oba Ukpolokpolo Erediauwa, oba of Benin; High Priest Osemwegie Ebohon; the Seattle Art Museum; Museum für Völkerkunde Vienna, Kunsthistorisches Museum; the Smithsonian Institution, National Museum of African Art; and an anonymous American private collection.

KATHLEEN BICKFORD BERZOCK
CURATOR OF AFRICAN ART
THE ART INSTITUTE OF CHICAGO

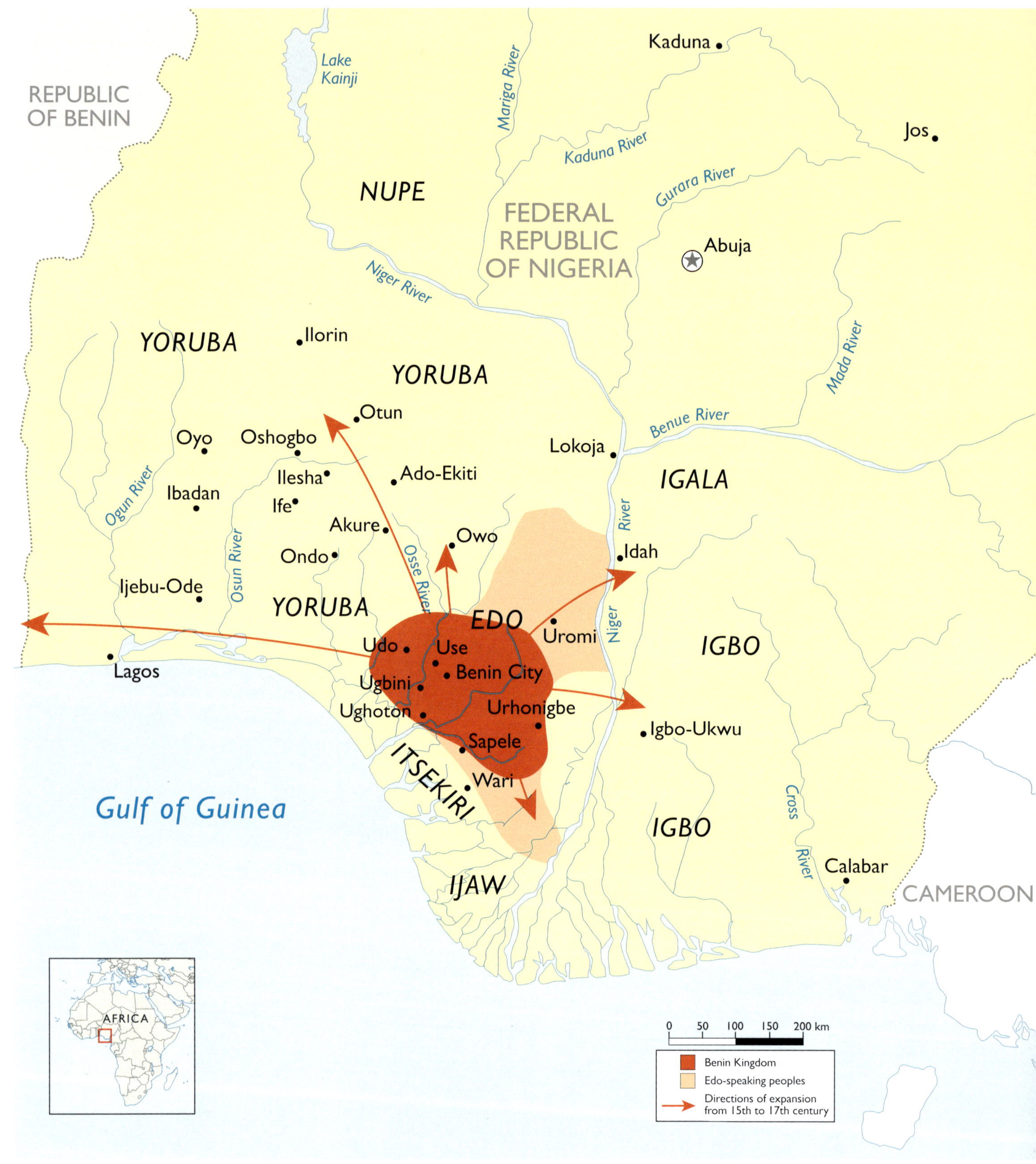


Fig. 1 Map of south-central Nigeria showing the Benin Kingdom.

The royal arts of the Benin Kingdom elaborate the centrality of the *oba*, the divine king, in multiple, richly nuanced ways. They affirm his authority and portray his divinity. They record the kingdom's significant historical events and the oba's involvement in them. They indicate rank within the court's hierarchy and signal the oba's sanction. And, they activate his interactions with the supernatural and honor his deified ancestors, forging a continuity that is vital to the kingdom's well-being.

The imagery of Benin's royal arts is multivalent and the media—primarily brass, ivory, and coral—are endowed with sacred power. The innate value of these materials within Benin, and the time and skill that is invested in working them, reflects the earthly and otherworldly influence of the oba and the great wealth of his kingdom. Benin's royal arts belong to a tradition that favors convention even as it promotes creativity and innovation, especially as a reflection of royal prerogative. Through time rulers have used the arts to interpret the history of the kingdom and to orient themselves with the past in an effort to support their own initiatives and define their own images for posterity.

The history of the Benin Kingdom stretches back to the thirteenth century. Located in the tropical forest region of south-central Nigeria, the kingdom coincides roughly with the modern Edo State (see fig. 1). The majority of its population is Edo; however, other peoples including Igbo, Ijaw, Yoruba, and Itsekiri also live within and along its borders.[1] In 1897 the British invaded the kingdom, forced the oba into exile, and stripped the palace of its royal arts. This decisive event irrevocably changed Benin's trajectory, though it did not destroy the kingdom. Today, the reigning oba of Benin, Omo n'Oba Ukpolokpolo Erediauwa (enthroned 1979), oversees administrative and ritual affairs from a large palace complex with the assistance of chiefs (see fig. 2), court officials, attendants, religious specialists, and family members. Under his guidance, the Edo people maintain a strong cultural identity within the Federal Republic of Nigeria and beyond.

## ROYAL ARTISTS

Strong patronage of the arts has characterized Benin's monarchy since its inception. The arts are necessary to many of the important royal practices, including outfitting ancestral altars and providing ceremonial implements and regalia for the oba and his court. Artists in the oba's employ belong to hereditary guilds that are administered within the Iwebo palace society, one of three groups that structure the complex organization of the court.[2] Until the twentieth century, guild members worked exclusively within the palace compound, allowing the oba to more fully oversee their labor and materials. This was particularly important for brass, ivory, and coral, valuable commodities that were controlled by sumptuary laws.

Brass casters (*igun eronmwon*) are the highest-ranking craft guild within the hierarchical structure of the Iwebo society, followed by blacksmiths (*igun ematon*) and ivory and wood carvers (*igbesanmwan*). Some of the other craft guilds affiliated with the society are weavers (*owina n'ido*), leather workers (*isekpoki*), and bead makers (*enisen*), who are in charge of crafting the coral and red stone regalia worn by the oba and, with his permission, by titleholders, chiefs, and others connected with the court.[3]

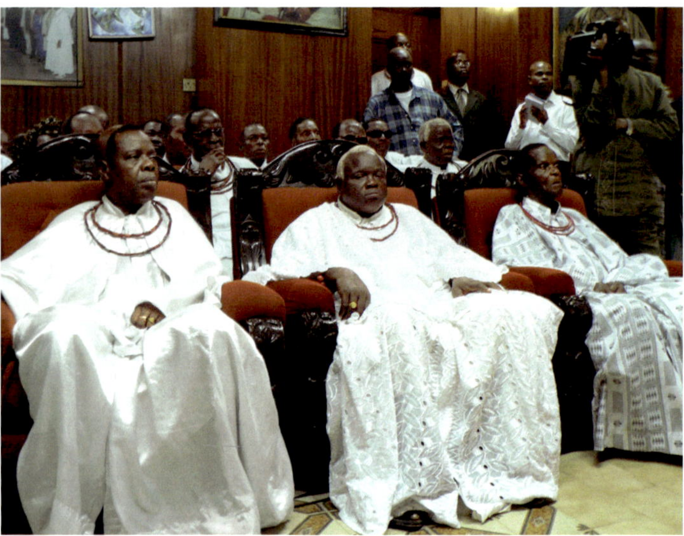

Fig. 2 High-ranking palace chiefs at a meeting in the reception room of the royal palace. Benin City, 2006. Photo by Wilfried Seipel.

### CHRONOLOGY OF THE OBAS OF BENIN

| | | | | | |
|---|---|---|---|---|---|
| 1 | Eweka I | c. 1200 | 20 | Ahenzae | c. 1641 |
| 2 | Uwakhuahen | | 21 | Akenzae | c. 1661 |
| 3 | Ehenmihen | | 22 | Akengboi | c. 1669 |
| 4 | Ewedo | c. 1255 | 23 | Akenkpaye | c. 1675 |
| 5 | Oguola | c. 1280 | 24 | Akengbedo | c. 1684 |
| 6 | Edoni | c. 1295 | 25 | Oreoghene | c. 1689 |
| 7 | Udagbedo | c. 1299 | 26 | Ewuakpe | c. 1700 |
| 8 | Ohen | c. 1334 | 27 | Ozuere | c. 1712 |
| 9 | Egbeka | c. 1370 | 28 | Akenzua I | c. 1713 |
| 10 | Orobiru | | 29 | Eresoyen | c. 1735 |
| 11 | Uwaifiokun | | 30 | Akengbuda | c. 1750 |
| 12 | Ewuare | c. 1440 | 31 | Obanosa | c. 1804 |
| 13 | Ezoti | c. 1473 | 32 | Ogbebo | c. 1816 |
| 14 | Olua | c. 1473 | 33 | Osemwende | c. 1816 |
| 15 | Ozolua | c. 1481 | 34 | Adolo | c. 1850 |
| 16 | Esigie | c. 1504 | 35 | Ovonramwen | c. 1888–1897 |
| 17 | Orhogbua | c. 1550 | 36 | Eweka II | 1914 |
| 18 | Ehengbuda | c. 1578 | 37 | Akenzua II | 1933 |
| 19 | Ohuan | c. 1608 | 38 | Erediauwa | 1979–present |

Fig. 3 Chronology of the obas of Benin, compiled by Joseph Egharevba. The dates of enthronement of the obas before 1700 are speculative.

Today the work of Benin's royal artists—in particular its brass casters and ivory carvers—is widely known, though much of its historic context and chronology is only a matter of speculation. The origins of brass casting in Benin are debated. One popular story credits Oba Oguola (enthroned c. 1280) with sending to Ile-Ife, the capital city of the ancient Ife Kingdom to the northwest, for a master brass caster to teach the craft, and with later establishing a royal brass-casting guild.[4] Others suggest brass casting developed independently in Benin and may have mutually benefited from exchange with Ile-Ife.[5] Casters in both regions use the lost-wax method, in which a precisely detailed wax model is formed over a clay core (see fig. 4). When the model is complete, clay is carefully applied over the wax. It is then heated, melting the wax, which exits from a narrow channel. Next, molten metal is poured into the mold. Once cool, the hardened clay is chipped away, leaving behind the image, now cast in brass.[6]

Ivory and wood carvers use very similar tools and techniques, working down an unformed tusk or wood block with adzes and knives (see fig. 5). Because it is difficult to obtain, is highly valued, and shares sacred associations with the oba, elephant ivory is far more restricted than wood. Ivory is dense and hard with a uniform grain that is ideal for creating works of great delicacy and detail. Young ivory carvers must learn to master a repertoire of motifs that have been passed down through generations before they are considered fully trained. At times carvers work collectively to accomplish large works, such as elaborate, multi-image altar tusks.

### MYTHIC ORIGINS

According to oral traditions, in the ancient past Benin was ruled by the Ogiso, literally "Rulers of the Sky," who are associated today with mythic feats and failures. While one account explains that the first Ogiso was the son of Osanobua, the High God, another claims that he was chosen from among the finest local rulers and that he governed to some extent through the good will of the people.[7] Contesting stories also recount the modern history of the Benin Kingdom (see fig. 3). The predominant one suggests that as the leadership of the Ogiso failed, the village chiefs of Benin, known collectively as *uzama*, sent a messenger to Ile-Ife asking its divine ruler, or *ooni*, for a leader to restore order. The ooni sent his son, Oranmiyan, to Benin. Oranmiyan was unhappy there and returned home,

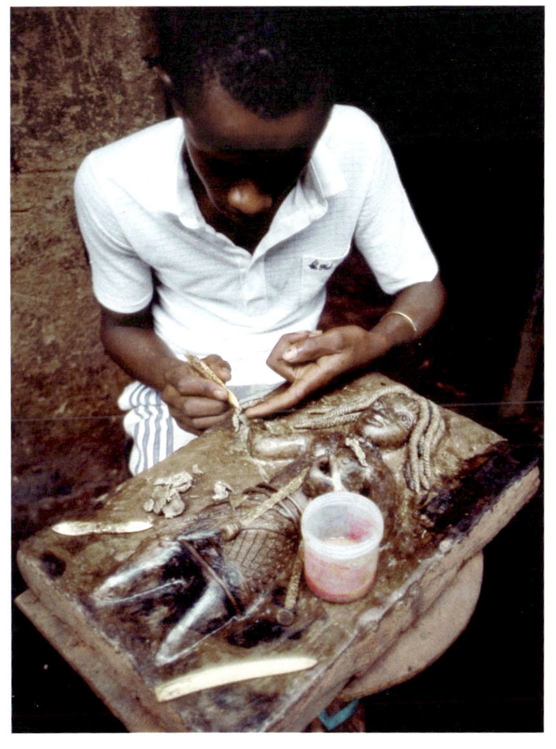

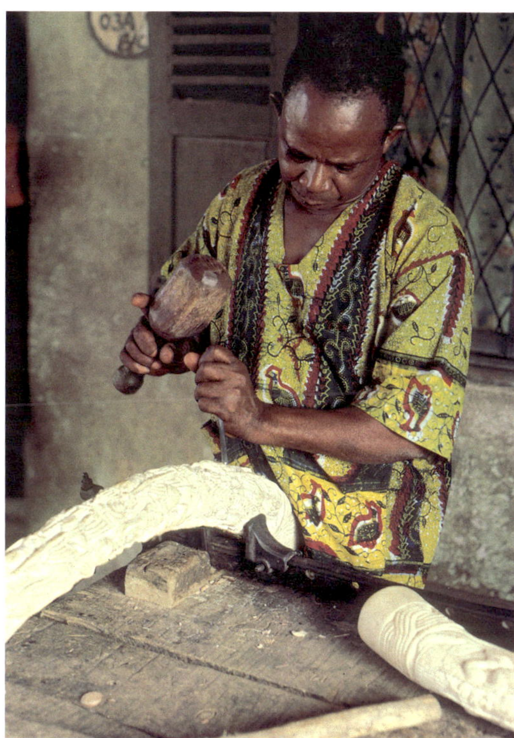

Fig. 4 A brass caster of the Omodamwen family workshop completes the wax model for a plaque. Benin City, 1992. Photo by Joseph Nevadomsky.

Fig. 5 Chief David Omoregie works on an ivory tusk commissioned by Oba Erediauwa. Benin City, 1991. Photo by Barbara W. Blackmun.

but not before conceiving a child with the daughter of an Edo village chief. Their son inherited the throne and was crowned Oba Eweka I around 1200.[8] An alternative tradition tells of a banished prince of Benin who arrived at Ile-Ife and became its king due to his extraordinary powers. When the Edo sought a ruler, they sent to Ile-Ife to ask for the return of their lost heir, who instead sent his son, Oranmiyan, to rule Benin.[9]

Scholars have pointed out the complexities and contradictions that these stories illuminate. Are the rulers of Benin of foreign origin, or are the leaders of Ife descended from an Edo prince? Did a divine oba impose his will upon the people, or was the oba's authority created to some extent through the people's temporal actions? Regardless, both versions emphasize a connection between the rulers of Benin and Ife and underscore the interdependency of the oba and the village chiefs, a relationship that provides checks and balances to power which are essential to the success and longevity of Benin's political system.

A symbolic focus on the head as the locus of human destiny also links Benin and Ife. In Benin the oba's head is worshiped as the source of the kingdom's well-being, and compelling evidence suggests that this is also the case in ancient Ife.[10] It is interesting to consider as well the prominent role of brass casting and its relationship to kingship practices in Ife and Benin, in particular the creation of lost-wax cast heads to commemorate rulers and what they may suggest about the kingdoms' shared history. Like the heads cast in Benin (see cat. 1), the Ife heads (see cat. 2) may have functioned as altar sculpture, though this remains speculative.

## OBA EWUARE AND THE PORTUGUESE

Benin's status as a regional powerhouse coalesced in the fifteenth century under the leadership of Oba Ewuare (enthroned c. 1440). Ewuare was responsible for many innovations that define and give structure to Benin kingship, including improvements to the royal capital, Benin City; the establishment of the three associations of palace chiefs; and the creation of an annual cycle of royal rituals to protect and renew the kingdom, including Ugie Erha Oba, which honors the oba's sacred ancestors, and Igue, which strengthens the oba's divine powers.[11]

Benin's position was fortified with the arrival of the Portuguese late in Ewuare's reign, and he is the first oba to be linked with the wealth and power that derived from coastal trade.[12] In Edo oral history, Ewuare is credited with obtaining the royal garments of coral beads (*ivie ebo*) and red flannel cloth (*ododo*) that were among the luxury goods imported to Benin. According to legend, Ewuare traveled to the palace of Olokun, the god of the waters and prosperity, and stole the deity's spiritually charged coral garments (see cats. 3–4 and fig. 6). This story may be a veiled reference to the arrival of the Portuguese, which brought the kingdom access to new forms of wealth.[13] In Benin's visual arts, the Portuguese are strongly associated with Olokun. They frequently appear alongside mudfish, crocodiles, snakes, and other beings that traverse between water and land, a trait shared by Portuguese seafaring merchants (see cat. 6).

A plaque depicting an oba whose legs take the form of electric mudfish (cat. 5) likewise refers to the oba's connection with Olokun. The extraordinary abilities of the electric mudfish, a variety of catfish that delivers a shock if touched and can exist out of water for extended periods of time, makes it a fitting symbol of the oba's otherworldly, terrifying powers. The fish-legged oba is depicted draped in coral regalia and often wears a faceted stone bead (*ivie egbo*) at the center of his chest (see cat. 4).[14] Deep red in color, the bead is among the emblematic symbols of Benin's monarchy.

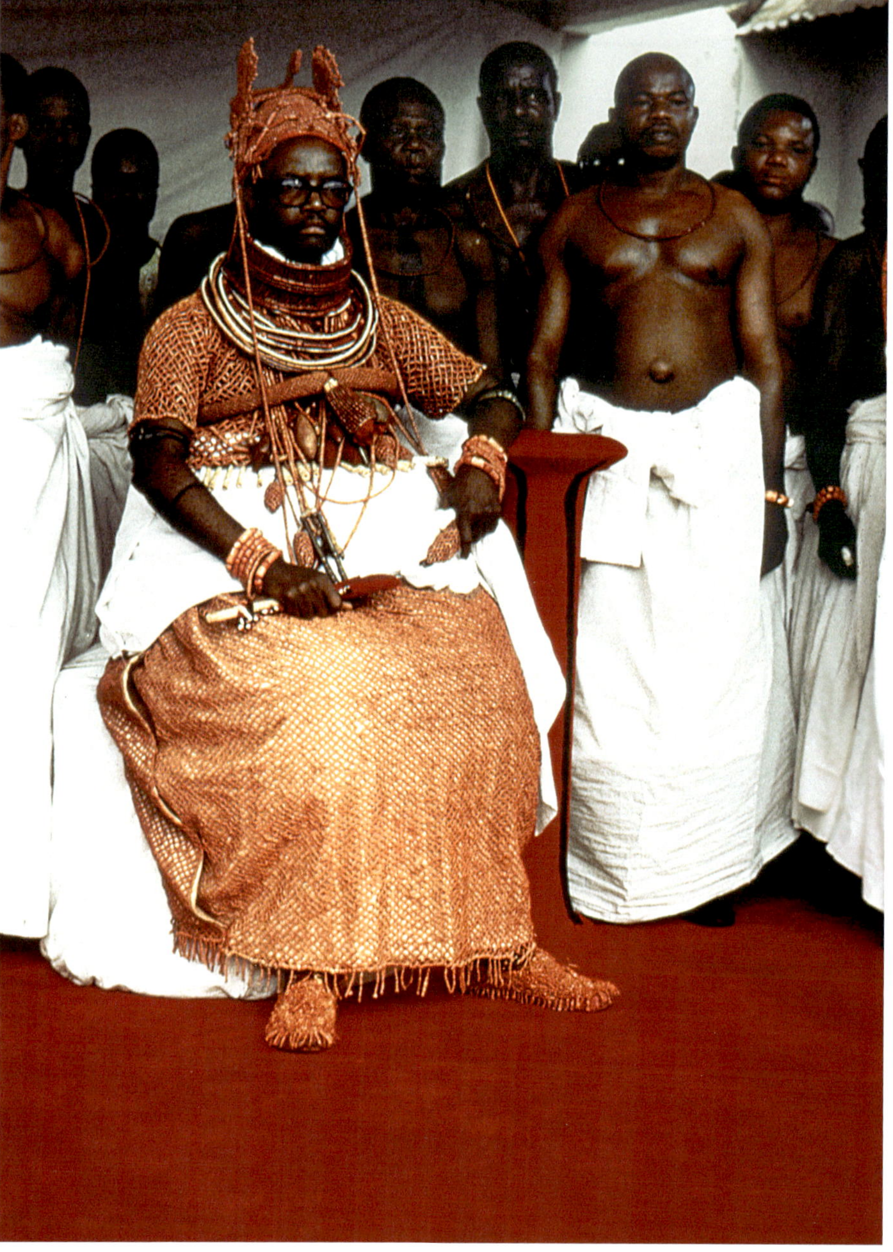

Fig. 6 Oba Erediauwa elaborately dressed in coral regalia during the Igue festival. Benin City, 1984. Photo by Joseph Nevadomsky.

## THE WARRIOR OBAS: OZOLUA AND ESIGIE

The fifteenth and sixteenth centuries are referred to as Benin's Golden Age. Oba Ozolua the Conqueror (enthroned c. 1481) and his heir, Oba Esigie (enthroned c. 1504), were strategic in using the growing wealth and might of the kingdom to expand its boundaries. As his appellation suggests, Ozolua had a passion for battle and actively pursued neighboring territories (see cat. 7).[15] Images of Ozolua on palace plaques (see cat. 8) and altar tusks celebrate the greatness of Benin, but they are also cautionary, as it was Ozolua's lust for battle that led to his demise. After years of almost constant military campaigning, Ozolua's closest friend, Laisolobi, caused the oba's death in order to allow his exhausted troops to return home.

The extent of Ozolua's interactions with the Portuguese is unclear; however, he certainly recognized their potential as a source of wealth and political clout, for he arranged to have a Portuguese tutor for his son Esigie.[16] As oba, Esigie embodied the great innovative spirit of Benin kingship, while also drawing on the influence of the Portuguese. He integrated Portuguese merchants and missionaries into the daily life of Benin City, and mimicking his own upbringing, he established a school where boys were taught to read and write Portuguese.[17] The square-cross motif, which predates the arrival of the Portuguese in Benin, was expanded in Esigie's reign and conflated with the cross of the Order of Christ.[18] It is found as a background pattern on a small group of plaques (see cat. 6) and, most prominently, is worn as a pendant by *ohensa* priests and *ewua* officials, who are members of a royal guild that was introduced by Esigie (see cat. 9).

Oba Esigie carefully regulated trade with the Portuguese and created a guild of commissioned traders to act as his emissaries (see cat. 10). Benin's earliest exports were Guinea pepper and slaves and later shifted to ivory, cotton and raffia textiles, and beads. In the nineteenth century, after the prohibition of

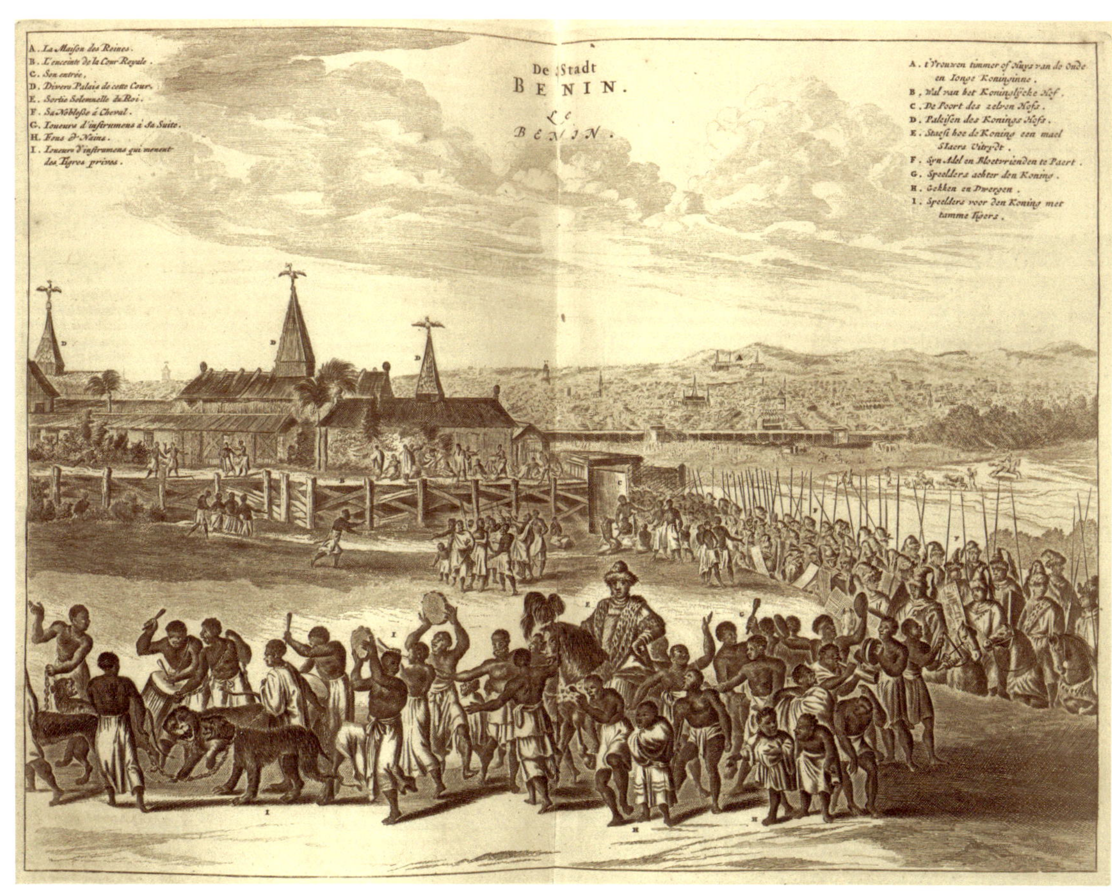


Fig. 7 A view of Benin City, from Olfert Dapper, *Naukerige Beschrijvinge der Africaensche gewesten*. Amsterdam, 1668. © British Library, London. All Rights Reserved. The British Library Board. Licence Number: ARTINS03.

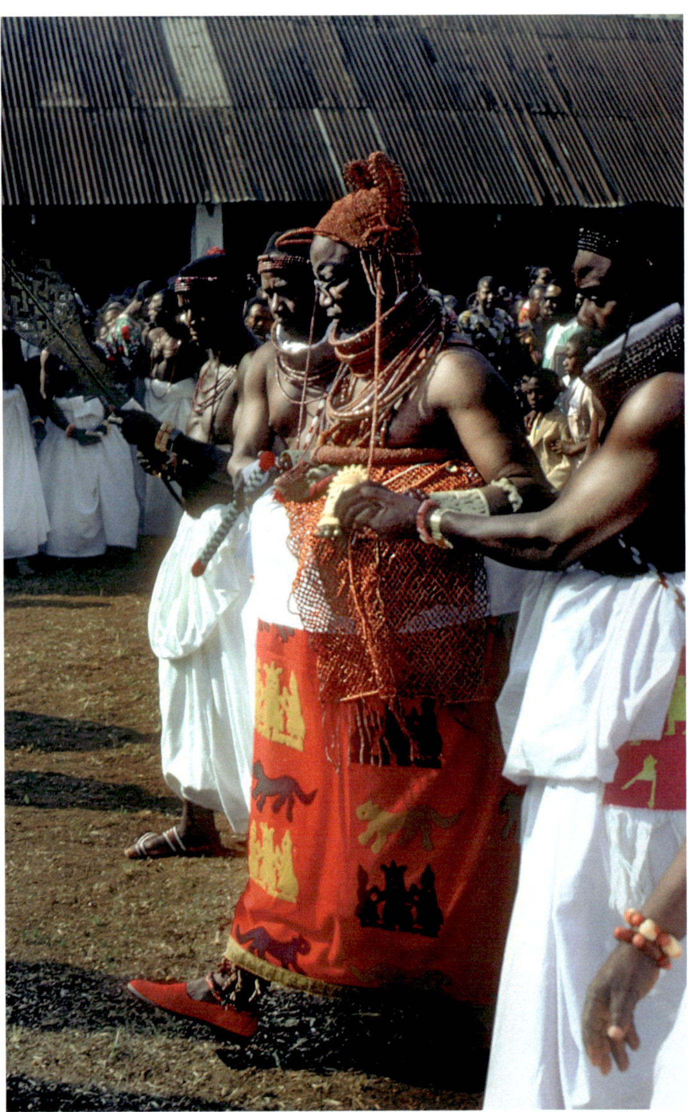

Fig. 8 Oba Erediauwa holds a hip pendant depicting Iyoba Idia as he participates in a ceremony during Igue. Benin City, 1985. Photo by Joseph Nevadomsky.

transatlantic slavery, palm oil and rubber became Benin's major exports. Throughout, Edo craftsmen also produced a variety of elaborately sculpted objects to suit the tastes of a luxury market abroad (see cat. 11).[19] In exchange, the Portuguese and later the Dutch, French, and English offered brass and a variety of manufactured goods from Europe, as well as exotic imports such as coral and cowrie shells.

Capitalizing on the influx of brass that came with coastal trade, Esigie increased his patronage of the royal guild of brass casters and commissioned them to make plaques to decorate his palace.[20] The plaques commemorate obas and the significant events of their reigns and record the hierarchy and ceremony of court life. One plaque (cat. 12), illustrating an interior courtyard or altar, suggests the manner in which these objects were aligned on the palace's pillars. According to the Dutch writer Olfert Dapper (see fig. 7), the palace complex "contains beautiful long square galleries…resting on wooden pillars, covered from top to bottom with cast copper, on which deeds of war and battle scenes are carved."[21] The production of plaques is believed to have ceased by the eighteenth century as internal struggles weakened the monarchy. In 1897, when the British invaded Benin City, hundreds of dusty plaques were found stored on the floor of one of the palace courtyards.[22]

Oba Esigie was aided by Portuguese mercenaries in battles that ultimately bolstered the kingdom and consolidated power under the oba. On palace plaques and altar tusks, he is frequently depicted on horseback, a pose emblematic of victory that also evokes his close relationship to the Portuguese (see cat. 13).[23] Esigie had another alliance that proved invaluable to him in wartime: his mother, Idia, used her deep knowledge of the occult to create protective and strengthening medicines for his soldiers and actively commanded her own army in battle. To honor Idia, Esigie created the title of *iyoba*, or queenmother, and endowed the position with rights, privileges, and responsibilities that are more typically associated with men (see fig. 8). The iyoba has her own palace in Uselu, and she keeps a full court with titled chiefs and attendants, receives tribute from villages in her domain, and wears chiefly regalia to conduct or attend rituals (see cat. 14).[24] Upon the iyoba's death, the oba commissions a commemorative brass head in her honor and establishes an altar in his palace that is decorated with artworks which forge a lasting connection to her spirit and elaborate her status (see cat. 15).

## INTERNAL CONFLICT AND RITUAL INTENSIFICATION

The Benin Kingdom's Golden Age ended when Oba Ohuan (enthroned c. 1608) died without an heir. Ensuing conflicts over succession weakened the control of Benin's monarchy, and powerful chiefs assumed much of the kingdom's administration. They also took on the responsibility of selecting a new ruler from among the male relatives of a

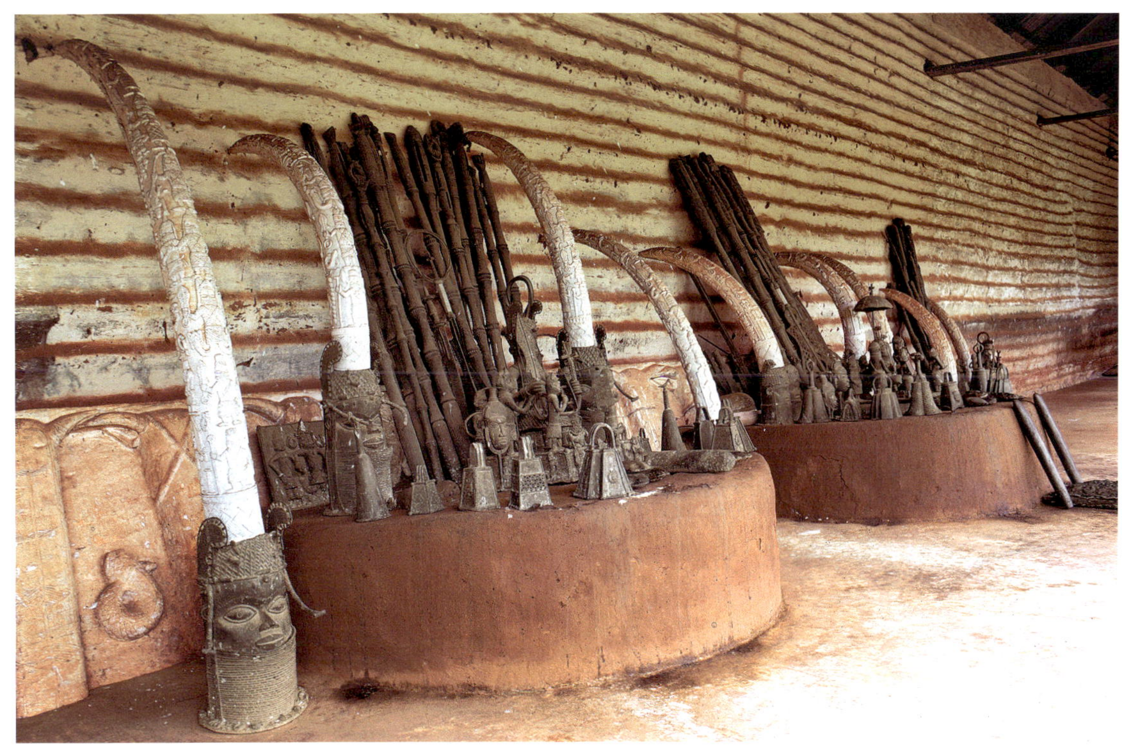

Fig. 9 The ancestral altars for Oba Ovonramwen (foreground) and Oba Eweka II (background). Benin City, 1970. Photo by Eliot Elisofon. Eliot Elisofon Photographic Archives, National Museum of African Art, Smithsonian Institution, photo no. EEPA EECL 7595.

deceased oba. In the following century, a series of puppet obas were enthroned in this fashion and ruled under the strong influence of the chiefs. In the last decades of the seventeenth century, however, Oba Ewuakpe (enthroned c. 1700) challenged this state of affairs.

Oral traditions relate that during Ewuakpe's reign a popular rebellion, perhaps stimulated by the controlling chiefs, protested his rule. He was stripped of his royal powers, including his coral regalia, and forced to leave Benin City.[25] Through perseverance and with support from the spirit realm, Ewuakpe made peace with the chiefs and returned to the throne.[26] An altar group (cat. 16) dramatizes the salient features of Ewuakpe's banishment and return to power.[27] The oba is pointedly depicted without his coral crown, the absence of which is underscored by his European-style helmet. The wrapper around his waist bears symbols of cosmic order and royal legitimacy, including a cross, a moon, a ceremonial sword, and a Portuguese head. He is flanked by two figures, whose body scarifications indicate that they are not Edo. It is possible that they are the slaves Ewuakpe purchased as he began his efforts to return from exile. Alluding to Ewuakpe's divine

ancestry, these figures stand holding his arms in a ritual pose of support. In his right hand, Ewuakpe grasps a pestle staff, a symbol of his ultimate reconciliation with the chiefs; his left hand holds a thunder axe, an object associated with the god of death that was believed to increase the potency of a curse or blessing delivered by the oba. Two decapitated human figures on the base of the altarpiece evoke the terrifying power of the oba, as only he could order a person's death. More specifically, they refer to the human sacrifices made by the oba at a series of annual rites culminating in Ugie Erha Oba, which honors his divine ancestry.

A related altar group (cat. 17) represents Ewuakpe's son, Oba Akenzua I (enthroned c. 1713).[28] Mirroring the altar group of Ewuakpe, Akenzua is depicted wearing a wrapper with cosmological signs and royal emblems; however, in contrast to Ewuakpe's foreign head covering and attendants, Akenzua wears layers of coral regalia and is supported under the arms by palace officials. At his feet are two leopards (see cat. 20), emblems of the oba's mastery over the regal beast, his counterpart in the wilderness. Like Ewuakpe, he holds a thunder axe in his left hand and a staff in his right. The imagery on Akenzua's staff speaks directly to his triumph over his brother, Ozuere, and his brother's powerful ally, Iyase n'Ode,[29] who challenged Akenzua's right to the throne. The staff depicts the oba standing on an elephant, a symbol of chiefly wealth and power that refers to Iyase n'Ode's reputation as a skilled magician who could transform himself into an elephant.

It has been suggested that the difficult struggles between obas and chiefs during the eighteenth century led the monarchy to accentuate the things that most differentiated them from the chiefs, namely their mystical abilities and divine ancestry.[30] Each oba took steps to increase the mysterious occult practices that connected them with the spirit realm and to strengthen their affinities to their most esteemed ancestors. It was in this era that the embellishment of royal altars was amplified (see cat. 18). The crowning of altar heads with massive, sculpted elephant tusks was also greatly enhanced (see fig. 9).[31] The increasing presence of ivory on royal altars also reflected a dramatic upsurge in its demand by Dutch merchants, who had replaced the Portuguese as the principal European traders along Africa's west coast. In the preceding centuries, ivory was strictly regulated by the oba, but with the change in trade partners and the increased demand, these regulations relaxed enough to allow Benin's wealthiest elite to wear ivory and place it on their ancestral altars (see cat. 19).[32]

## 1897: THE BRITISH INVASION OF BENIN

In the early nineteenth century, the British were Benin's primary trading partners; however, disputes over the control of trade led to strain.[33] This escalated in 1885, when the major European powers met in Berlin to brazenly divide Africa into colonial territories. Following the Berlin Conference, the British used force to accumulate land across the Niger Coast region, with Benin as the lone hold out. Things came to a head in January 1897, when a large British delegation led by the Acting Consul-General of the Niger Coast Protectorate, James Phillips, set off for Benin City despite multiple requests from Oba Ovonramwen (enthroned c. 1888) to postpone their visit. Willfully, and perhaps naïvely since Phillips had only recently arrived in the region, the Acting Consul-General ignored clear warnings from the oba and others that he was unavailable to receive visitors.[34]

On January 12, the British delegation was ambushed en route to Benin City by an Edo force that by all accounts acted without the oba's knowledge.[35] Almost the entire party was killed, including

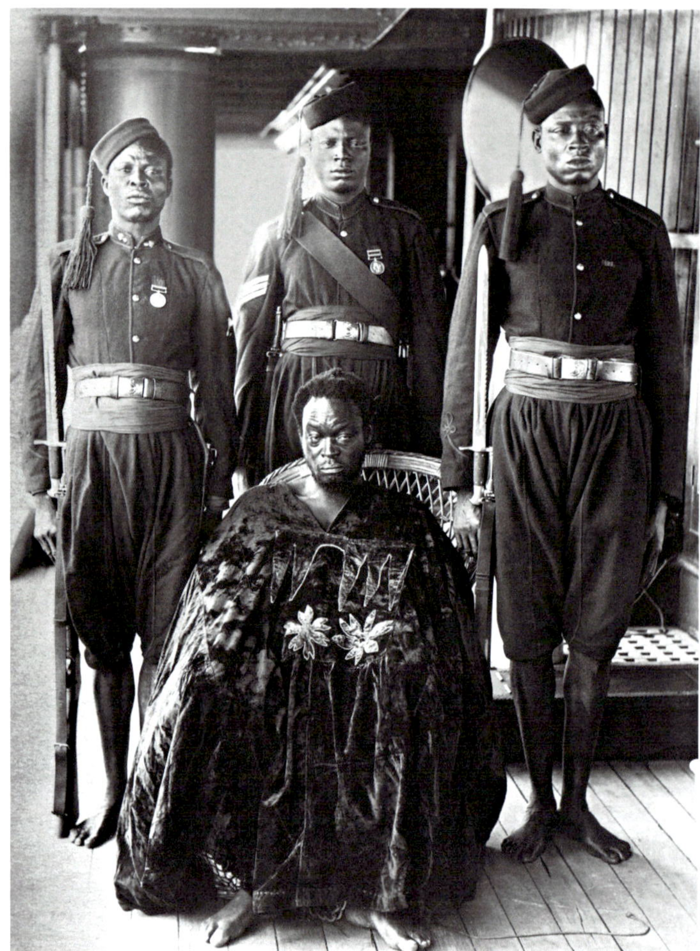

Fig. 10 Oba Ovonramwen on the British yacht *Ivy*, 1897. Photo courtesy of the Museum für Völkerkunde Wien, collection Maschmann, photo no. 6186.

Phillips. In quick order, a large British military force—deemed the Punitive Expedition—was assembled, and on February 18, 1897, they arrived in Benin City under orders to invade and conquer it. In time they captured Oba Ovonramwen and sent him to exile in Calabar, a city southeast of Benin (see fig. 10).[36]

With these dramatic events, the daily routines of the royal court and its cycle of rituals abruptly ceased. The Edo people were severed from the leaders that structured their kingdom and channeled its power. Adding to the calamity of the invasion, the possessions of the oba and his court were now the spoils of war. The objects were rounded up with little regard for their associative meaning (see fig. 11). No systematic record was kept of their groupings or placement; few inquiries were made as to their use, history, or content. Many of these objects were shipped to the London offices of the Admiralty for cataloging and were sold to help defray the costs of the invasion. Others were shared among members of the expeditionary force according to their rank.[37] Still others left Benin in the months and years after 1897, taken or sold in the confusion that followed the devastation of the kingdom.

Instantly upon their arrival in London, the objects were a topic of conversation and speculation, and at times were grossly misrepresented as "fetishes" made by a society in decay.[38] They sparked immediate interest from museums, particularly in Britain and the German-speaking world, and efforts were made in London, Oxford, Berlin, Dresden, Vienna, and elsewhere to purchase as many works as possible for public collections. Eventually art from Benin could be found in museums across Europe and the United States.[39]

## BENIN AFTER 1914: THE OBA'S RETURN

Oba Ovonramwen died in exile in 1914, the same year that the British returned his son to Benin City to be crowned Oba Eweka II. Benin's monarchy was thus restored, though with its power greatly curtailed.[40] While the Edo people maintained a strong connection to the oba, the structure of the kingdom was reconfigured to be secondary to the colonial system (see fig. 12), and, after 1963, to the government of the Federal Republic of Nigeria. Oba Eweka II and his successor, Oba Akenzua II (enthroned 1933), used the arts strategically in their efforts to reinvent the kingdom. Both obas commissioned carvers and casters to make works of art to replace those that were taken from the palace in 1897. In keeping with tradition, among Eweka's first acts was the establishment of an altar dedicated to his father, Oba Ovonramwen. He also erected a single collective altar dedicated to all of the deceased obas that had reigned before him. Eweka and Akenzua reinstated some of the royal rituals, though they reconsidered their role within a modern context. For instance, Eweka resumed the Igue festival in an abbreviated form, while Akenzua grouped its events within a two-week period in December for the practical reason of coinciding with the school holidays.[41] This celebration has

been further enhanced under the current leadership of Oba Erediauwa.

Since 1897 brass casting and ivory carving have been separated from the oba's exclusive control, though the guilds still regularly take royal commissions and reserve certain art forms exclusively for the oba.[42] Integration of the arts into the curriculum of secondary schools and universities has also nurtured and stimulated Benin's artistic traditions.[43] Building on Benin's long practice of commercialism, artists from the royal guilds are actively marketing their work nationally and internationally.[44] Many of Benin's royal artists find inspiration in re-examining themes addressed by their predecessors. Two recent works that depict Oba Ovonramwen's journey into exile demonstrate the far greater interpretive range that contemporary artists exercise. Both objects were produced in

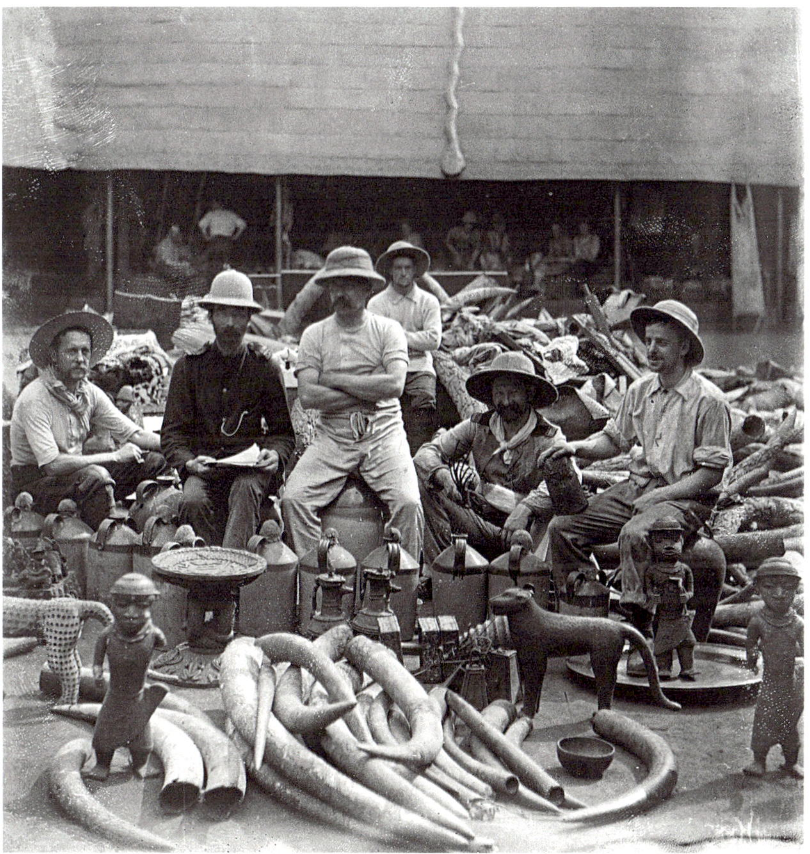

Fig. 11 Members of the British military expedition to Benin City pause for a photograph amid hundreds of artworks in a courtyard of the oba's palace. Benin City, 1897. © The Trustees of the British Museum, Af-CA 79-13.

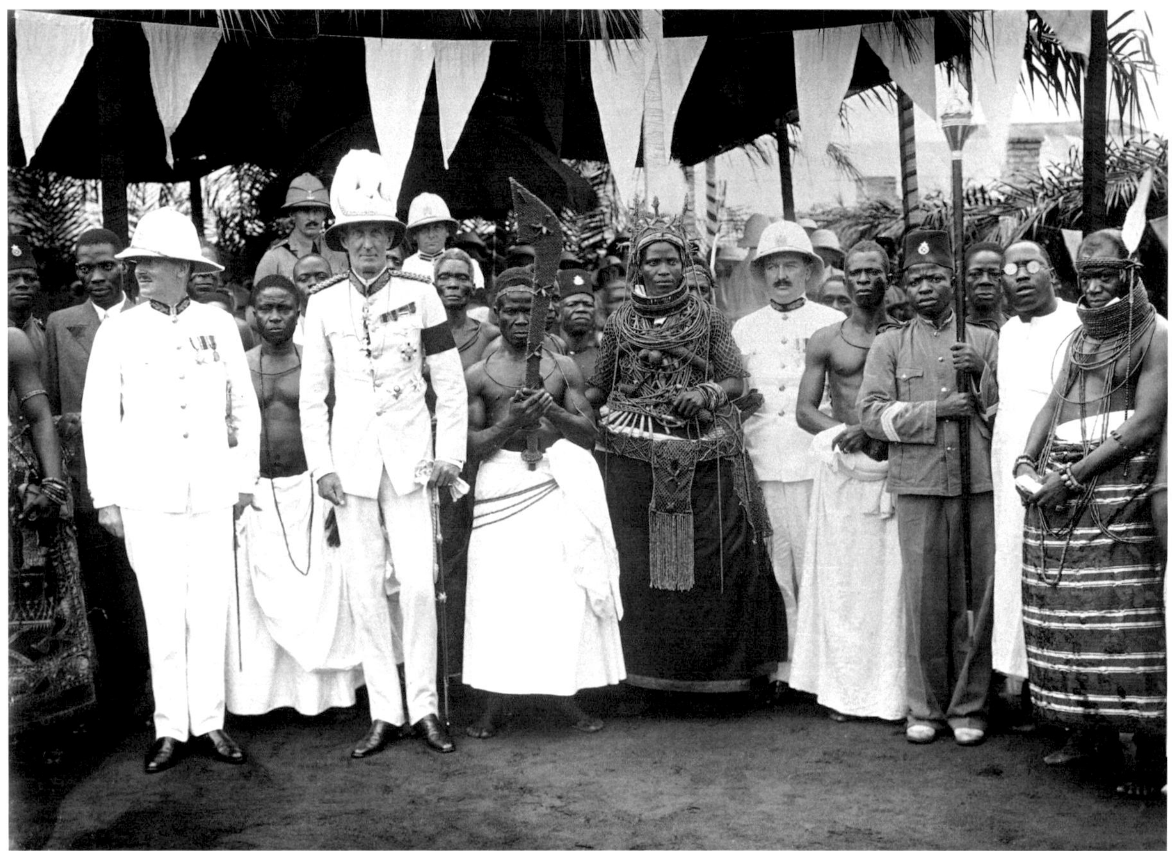

Fig. 12 Oba Akenzua II with British officials at Ugha Ozolua, October 9, 1936. © The Trustees of the British Museum, Af-A79-18.

the Omodamwen workshop, one of the most prominent brass-casting houses in Benin City. Philip Omodamwen's plaque (cat. 21) refers directly to the historic photograph of the event (fig. 10), portraying the oba as a tragic fallen hero stripped almost entirely of the props of kingship. In contrast, *Boat Composition* (cat. 22), a work by an unidentified member of the workshop, dramatically recasts Ovonramwen's experience, reclaiming for him and his people some of the dignity of his royal position.

In 1938, in a gesture of great significance to the Edo people, the British returned pieces of Oba Ovonramwen's revered coral regalia to his grandson Oba Akenzua II, thus restoring some of the sacred force of his ancestors. Upon receiving the regalia, Akenzua is said to have sung out with joy, "The poisonous arrow has killed the elephant," a reference to the long wait that is sometimes necessary before a victory can be attained.[45] For the Edo people, the royal arts of Benin retain the aura of royal prerogative and divine sanction that filled them with

meaning before the 1897 invasion. They have also attained global recognition as being among the great aesthetic traditions of the African continent. In the words of Nigerian artist and scholar Adepeju Layiwola, "These works do not only satisfy a psychological need [for Benin], but provide a deep sense of pride…for Africa and its Diaspora as a whole."[46]

**NOTES**

1. Edo is also spoken by the neighboring Ishan, Northern Edo, and Isoko; see Bradbury 1973, p. 48.
2. The other palace societies are Iweguae and Ibiwe; for more on royal guilds, see Inneh 2007.
3. For a more comprehensive list of guilds, see Plankensteiner 2007a, p. 104, fig. 2.
4. Egharevba 1968, p. 11; and Inneh 2007, p. 103. The current oba of Benin contradicts this tale, stating that it was the Edo who initiated brass casting and introduced it at Ife; personal communication with Plankensteiner, 2008; and Eweka 1992, p. 54.
5. Gore 1997, p. 55; and Inneh 2007, p. 105.
6. While some Benin castings are bronze (an alloy of copper and tin), the vast majority are leaded brass (an alloy of copper, lead, and zinc); the term "bronze" is sometimes used in the literature on Benin to identify an art-historical category of works cast in any of the copper alloys; see Plankensteiner 2007b.
7. See Igbafe 2007, pp. 41–42; see also Egharevba 1968, p. 1.
8. For a recounting of this story, see Egharevba 1968, pp. 6–7; Bradbury 1973, p. 44; and Ben-Amos 1995, p. 9.
9. See Igbafe 2007, p. 44.
10. See note 5.
11. Igbafe 2007, pp. 46–47; Ben-Amos 1995, pp. 32–34, 103; and Ben-Amos 1999, pp. 129–30; for a chart illustrating the organization of the palace societies, see Plankensteiner 2007a, p. 92, fig. 3.
12. Whether or not the explorer Ruy de Sequeira, sailing in 1472, reached the Benin Kingdom is a point of debate. João Afonso de Aveiro's visit to the kingdom in 1486 is documented. For a brief summary of these landmark events, see Bradbury 1973, p. 33; and Ryder 1969.
13. See Bradbury 1973, p. 34; Bradbury elaborates that Ewuare also initiated the Iwebo palace society, which is responsible for the making and care of royal regalia.
14. For more on the fish-legged oba motif, see Blackmun 1990.
15. Edo oral history claims that Ozolua's army conquered territory as far west as the Yoruba city of Ijebu-Ode.
16. Egharevba 1968, p. 28.
17. Archivo Nacional da Torre do Tombo, Lisbon, CCI-65-57, as cited in Blackmun 1990, p. 67.
18. Blackmun 2007c, p. 166; the Order of Christ was founded in Portugal in 1318 as a religious and military order. In the fifteenth century, under the leadership of Prince Henry the Navigator, it became a powerful military force for the Portuguese monarchy and was given autonomy over African coastal trade.
19. See Ben-Amos 1995, p. 37; and Ryder 1969, pp. 50–98, 124–281.

20. Esigie is believed to be the innovator of the plaque form in Benin; the form itself may have been inspired by Portuguese imports; see Ben-Amos 1995, p. 39.
21. Jones 1998, p. 71.
22. Today there are over 900 known plaques.
23. Nevadomsky 1986, p. 45; Alan Ryder reported that in 1505, King Manuel of Portugal sent a riding horse to the oba of Benin; Ryder 1969, pp. 40–50, as cited in Blackmun 2007b, p. 441.
24. Ben-Amos 1983, pp. 80–81; and Kaplan 2007, p. 145.
25. Today, the most common explanation for Ewuakpe's expulsion is that he exhausted the tolerance of his people when he ordered excessive human sacrifices to be made following the death of his mother; see Egharevba 1968, pp. 37–38; Paula Girshick Ben-Amos pointed out that this is far from definitive and suggested alternate explanations exist, including that the rebellion was caused by members of Ewuakpe's extended family, who challenged his selection as oba, or by the village chiefs, who wanted greater control of the kingdom; Ben-Amos 1999, pp. 42–43.
26. During Oba Ewuakpe's exile, a diviner told him that the spirit realm would support his desire to return to the throne only if he offered a human sacrifice. His faithful wife, Iden, volunteered herself, thus gaining this critical supernatural sanction; see Ben-Amos 1999, p. 82.
27. This reading of the Ewuakpe altar group is drawn from Ben-Amos Girshick 2007b, p. 470; and Ben-Amos 1999, pp. 83–92.
28. This reading of the Akenzua I altar group is drawn from Ben-Amos Girshick 2007a; and Ben-Amos 1999, pp. 96–101.
29. The iyase is Benin's highest-ranking village chief and a powerful military leader.
30. Ryder 1969, pp. 15–16; and Gallagher 1983, p. 81, as cited in Ben-Amos 1999, p. 69.
31. Blackmun 1991, p. 55; and Blackmun 2007c, pp. 161–62.
32. Blackmun 2007a.
33. See Igbafe 1970b for an enumeration and analysis of the events leading up to the British invasion of Benin.
34. The oba was engaged in the concluding rites of Auge, which required his seclusion for three Edo months (equivalent to six weeks). The successful completion of Auge was critical to the continued equilibrium of the kingdom; see Curnow 1997.
35. For more on these events, see Home 1982.
36. The oba and his chiefs fled Benin City before the attack and did not surrender until August; see Igbafe 1970b, p. 398; and Plankensteiner 2007c, p. 199.
37. Home 1982, as cited in Plankensteiner 2007b, pp. 32–33.

38. In his massive study *Die Altertümer von Benin* (1919), the Austrian scholar Felix von Luschan estimated that some 4,000 works could be found in collections across Europe by the early second decade of the twentieth century.
39. See Coombes 1994 for a careful analysis of the reception of these works in Britain; see Plankensteiner 2007c for a consideration of their reception in Germany and Austria. For a brief history of the acquisition of works from Benin in France and the United States in the 1930s and 1940s, see Paudrat 2007.
40. Igbafe 1970a.
41. Nevadomsky and Airihenbuwa 2007, p. 127.
42. Inneh 2007, p. 107.
43. Nevadomsky 1997, pp. 56–57.
44. Nevadomsky and Osemweri 2007, p. 257.
45. Layiwola 2007, p. 88.
46. Ibid., p. 87.

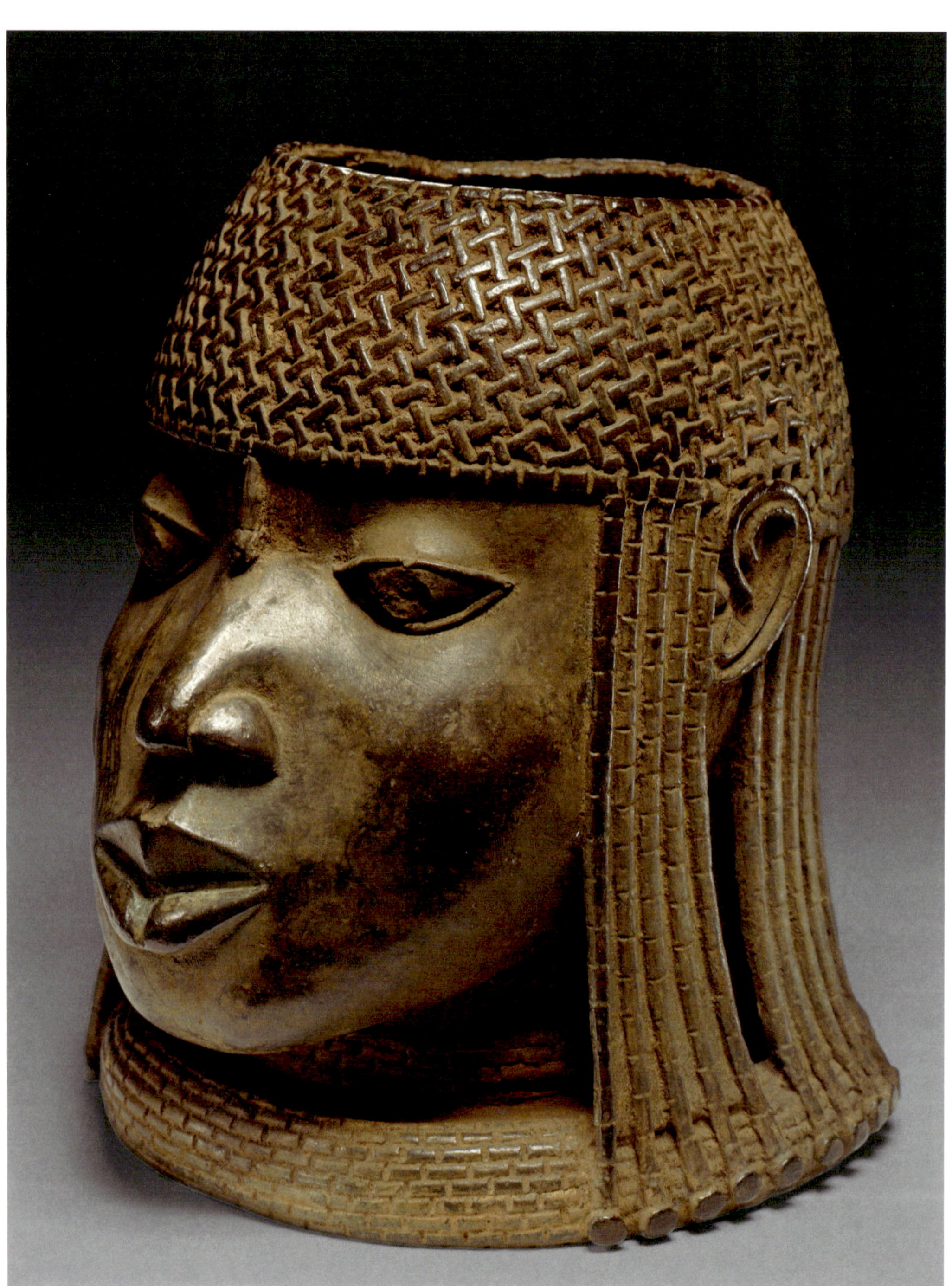

1.

**ALTAR HEAD OF AN OBA**
**(*UHUNMWUN ELAO*)**
Edo
Benin Kingdom, Nigeria
16th century
Brass; 20 x 19 x 22 cm
(7 ⅞ x 7 ½ x 8 ⅝ in.)
Staatliche Museen zu Berlin,
Ethnologisches Museum, III C 8169

Benin's royal altar heads appear in a range of styles from highly formalized to the more idealized naturalism of this example. Works such as this head, with its distinctive roll of beadwork at the neck and beaded strands hanging from the crown, are believed to date to the sixteenth century. It is possible that the naturalism of this style may reflect a connection with the brass-casting traditions of the Ife Kingdom (see cat. 2).

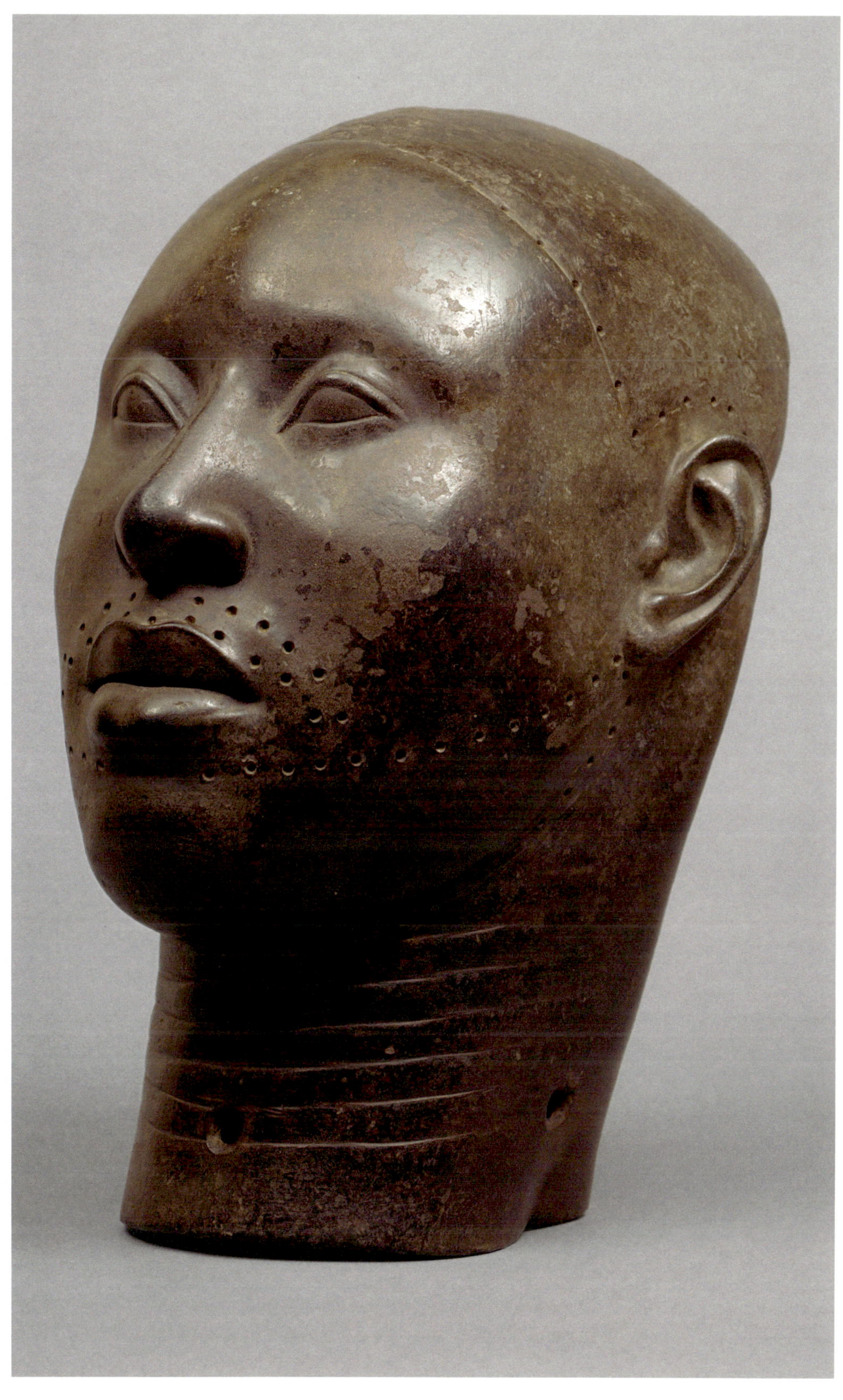

2.
**HEAD**
Ife
Nigeria
12th/15th century
Brass; 31 x 25 x 19 cm
(12 ³⁄₁₆ x 9 ⅞ x 7 ½ in.)
The National Commission for
Museums and Monuments, Nigeria,
1999.2.3

According to some oral traditions, Benin traces its modern origins to the ancient city of Ile-Ife, which was a thriving urban center by the eleventh century. Among the artworks that survive from the city are a number of idealized brass heads, including this magnificent work. Holes outlining the hairline, lip, and jaw were likely used to secure hair or beaded regalia to the head. Larger holes at the neck may have been used to attach it to a wood body, perhaps during burial rites. The Ile-Ife heads may also have been placed on altars, as are brass examples from Benin.

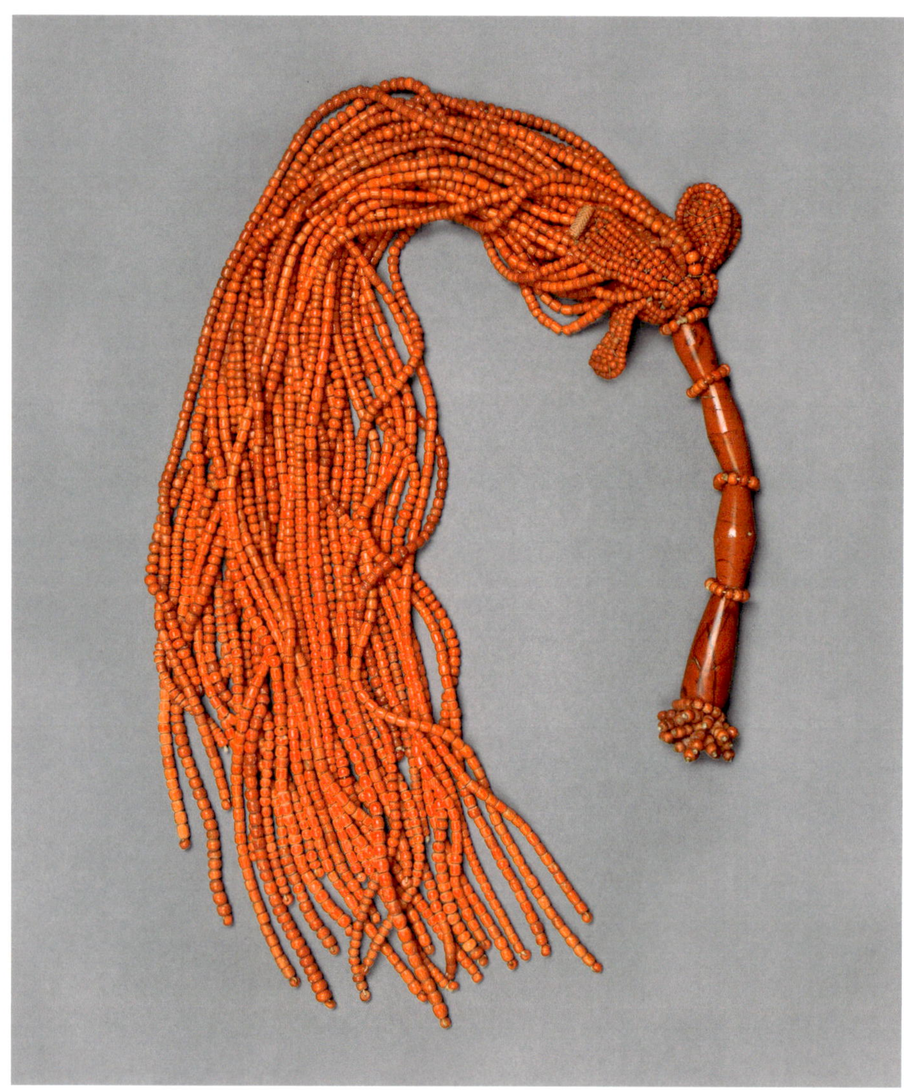

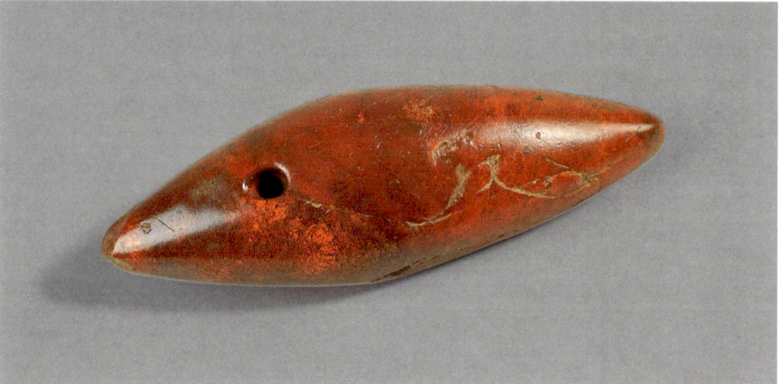

3–4.

## OBA'S FLY WHISK (*UGBUDIAN IVIE*)

Edo
Benin Kingdom, Nigeria
18th/19th century
Coral, agate, and copper; 99.5 x 10 x 4 cm
(39 ⅛ x 3 ¹⁵⁄₁₆ x 1 ⁹⁄₁₆ in.)
The Trustees of the British Museum, London,
Af1898, 0630.3

## OBA'S STONE BEAD (*IVIE EGBO*)

Edo
Benin Kingdom, Nigeria
18th/19th century
Jasper; 9.5 x 3 cm (3 ¾ x 1 ³⁄₁₆ in.)
Museum für Völkerkunde Dresden, Staatliche
Ethnographische Sammlungen Sachsen (SES),
18055

Regalia made of coral or red stone beads are
emblematic of the oba's divine rule. This elegant
coral fly whisk is a true luxury item, as its weight—
approximately five and a half pounds—makes
it altogether impractical to use. The oba's stone
bead (ivie egbo) is worn prominently at the center
of his chest (see cat. 5). Oral traditions tell of its
electrifying force, which will harm all but the
legitimate ruler.

5.

## U-SHAPED PLAQUE OF A FISH-LEGGED
## OBA WITH ATTENDANTS

Edo
Benin Kingdom, Nigeria
18th century (?)
Brass; 40 x 35.5 x 6.5 cm (15 ¾ x 14 x 2 ⁹⁄₁₆ in.)
Museum für Völkerkunde zu Leipzig, Staatliche
Ethnographische Sammlungen Sachsen (SES),
MAf 34550

This U-shaped plaque depicts a fish-legged oba.
Here, as in many versions of the motif, he wears
coral regalia and the oba's stone bead (ivie egbo)
at his chest (see cat. 4). Two attendants flank and
support his arms, suggesting the obligation of the
Edo people to support their leader and recalling
the great weight of the oba's divine power.

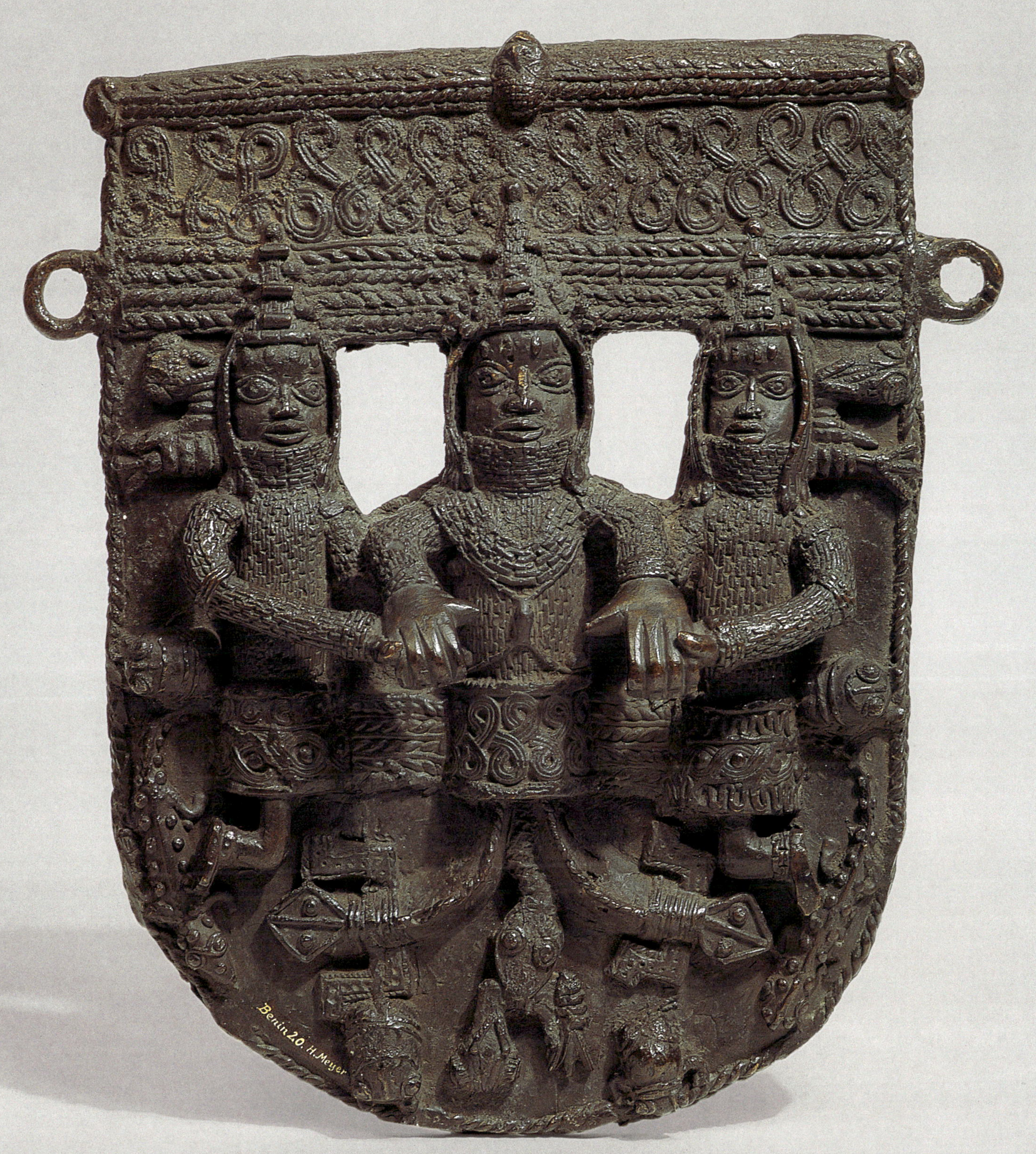
Benin 20. H.Meyer

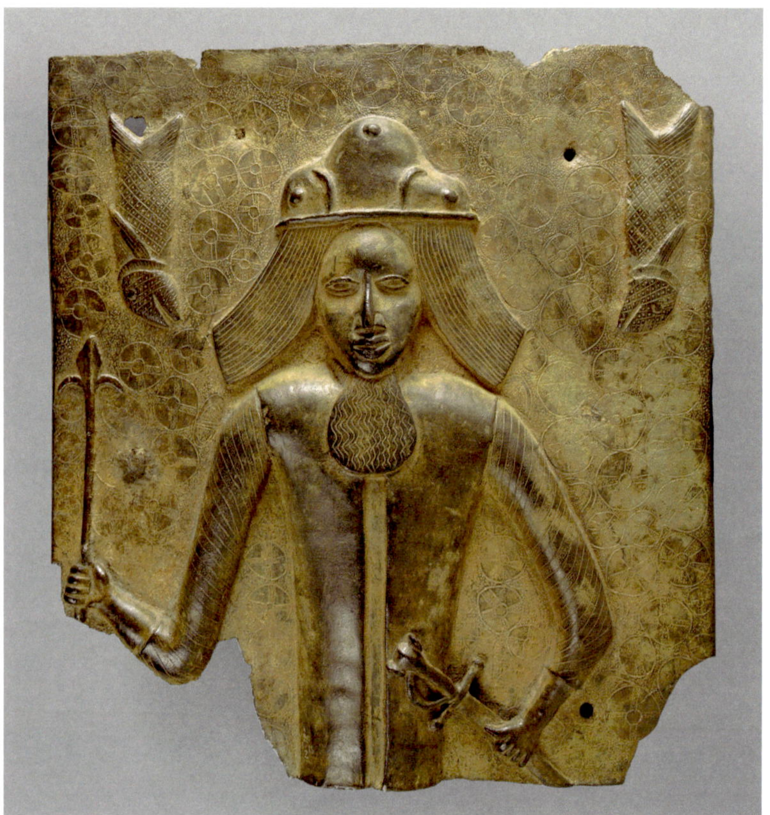

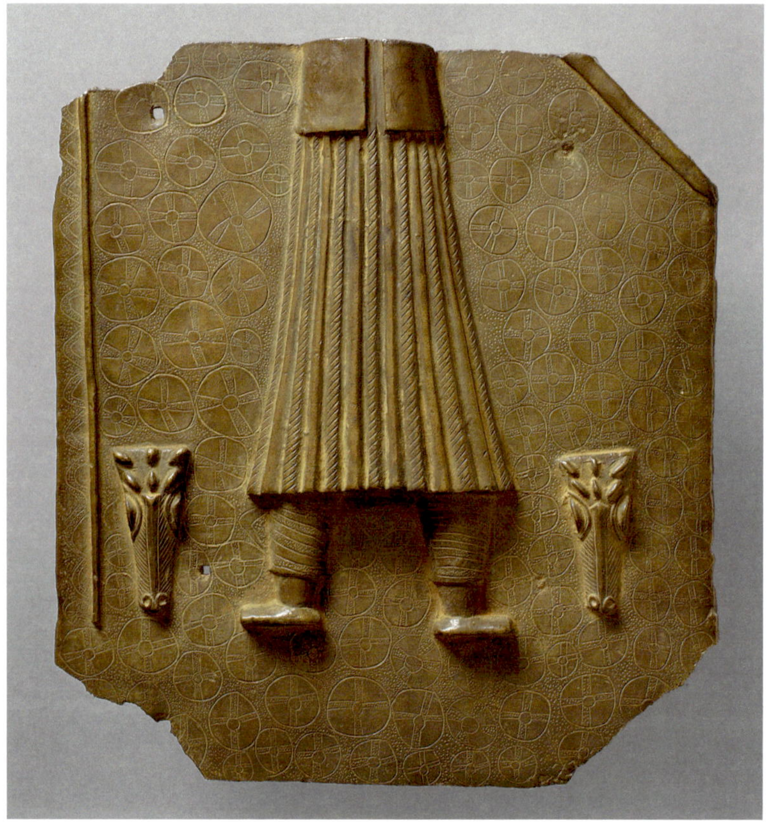

6.

## DOUBLE PLAQUE OF A PORTUGUESE MAN

Master of the Circled Cross (active 16th/17th century)
Edo
Benin Kingdom, Nigeria
16th/17th century
Brass
Top: 42.5 x 41.5 x 7.5 cm (16 ¾ x 16 ⅜ x 2 ⁵⁄₁₆ in.)
The Trustees of the British Museum, London, Af1898, 0115.2
Bottom: 40 x 38 x 6 cm (15 ¾ x 15 x 2 ⅜ in.)
Museum für Völkerkunde Wien, 64.718

In Benin's royal arts, Portuguese merchants and missionaries are frequently associated with powerful, dangerous creatures of the water, including mudfish (seen here in the upper corners) and crocodiles (lower corners). This work is one of a small number of double plaques that portray an image across two square panels. It is identified as the work of a sixteenth-century master brass caster whose style is distinguished by elongated figures and by the distinctive background motif of a circle around a square cross.

7.

## PLAQUE OF A BATTLE SCENE, POSSIBLY THE IDAH WAR

Benin Master (active 16th/17th century)
Edo
Benin Kingdom, Nigeria
16th/17th century
Brass; 55 x 39 cm (21 ⅝ x 15 ⅜ in.)
Museum für Kunst und Gewerbe Hamburg, 1899.75

In the corpus of Benin art, the six plaques that depict battle scenes are among the most complex and accomplished works. Here, a high-ranking Edo warrior—the largest figure in the composition—has slashed and mortally wounded a soldier on horseback, probably the leader of the opposing army. At the far right, another Edo soldier holds the severed head of a rival. The taking of trophy heads in battle was a feature of Edo warfare.

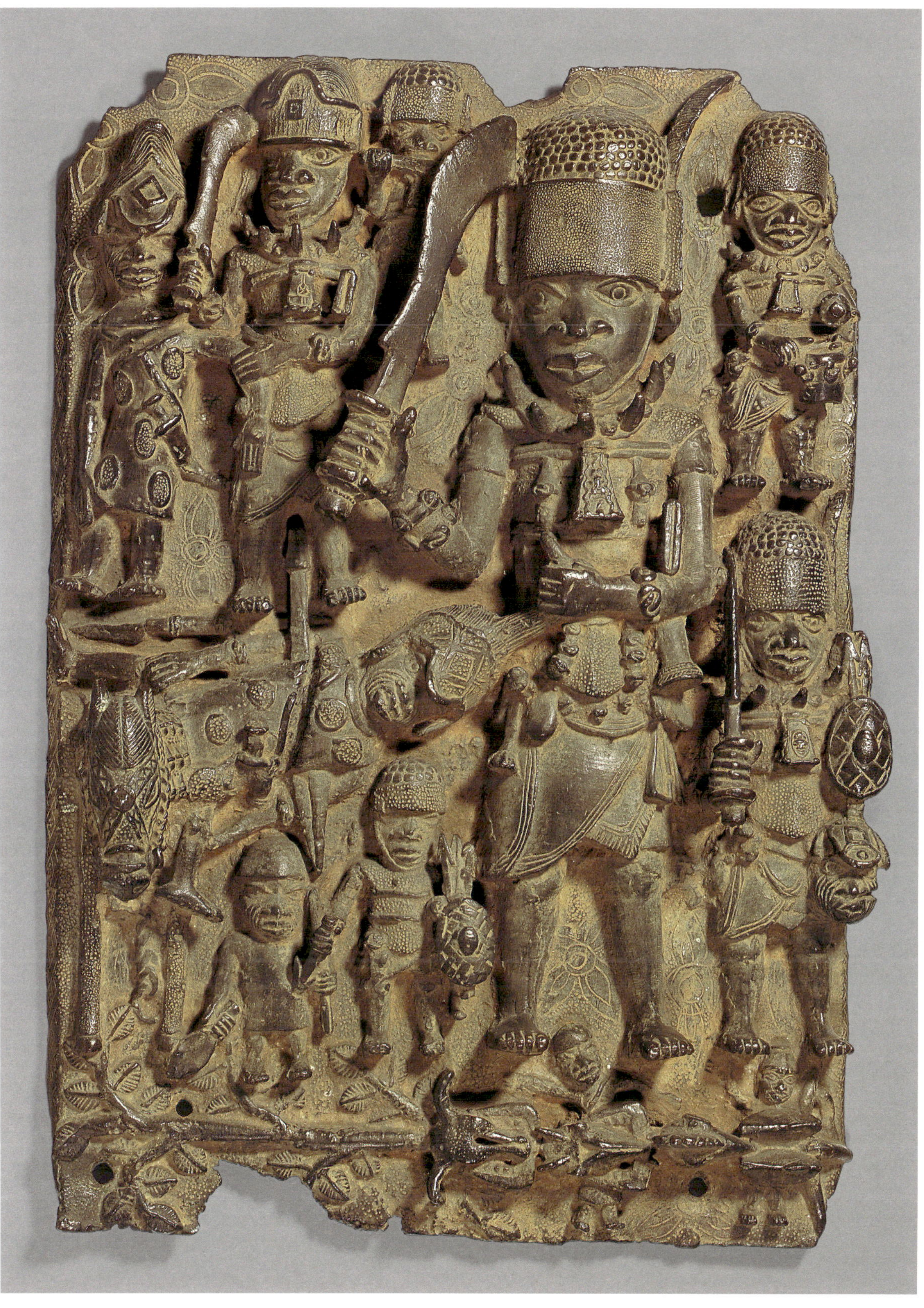

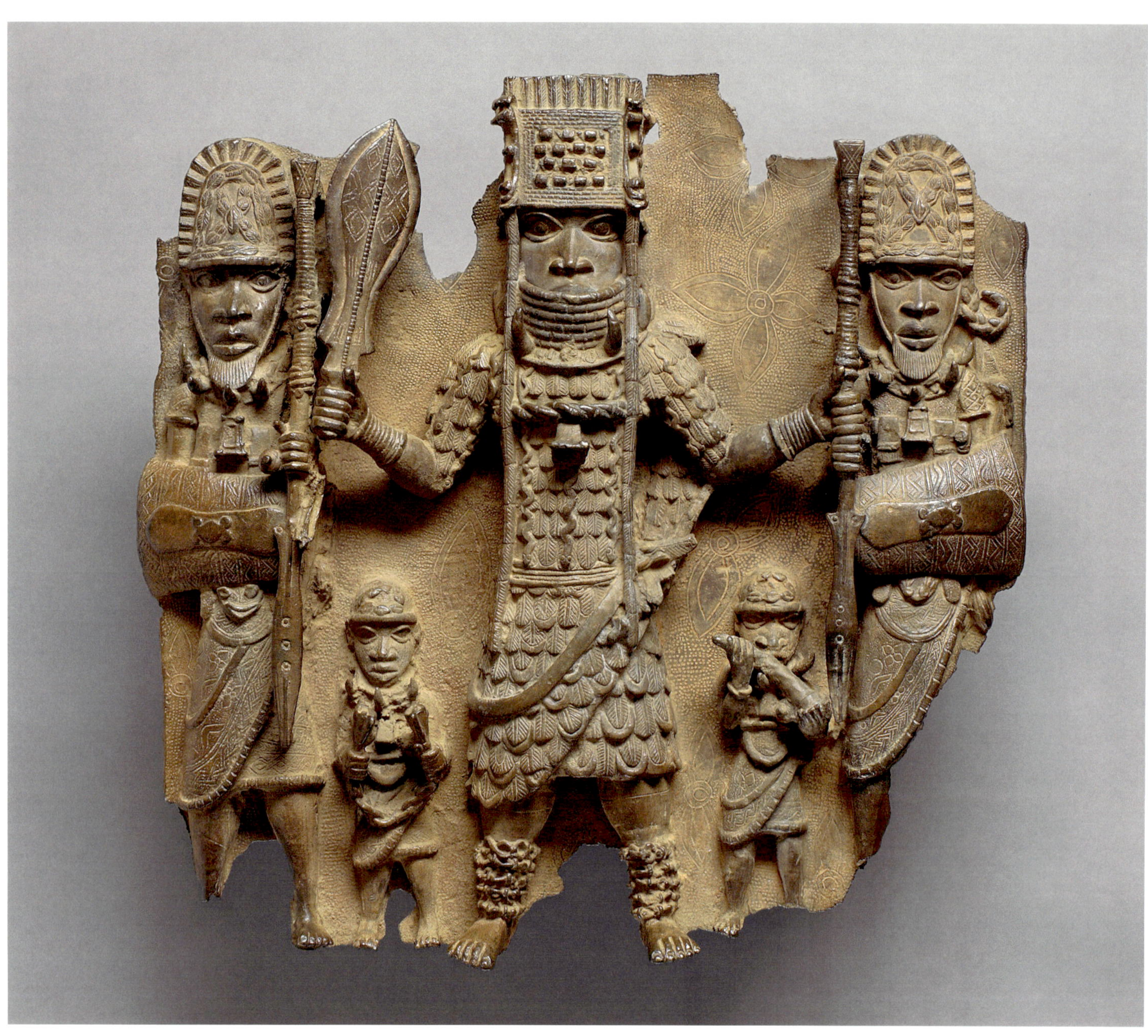

8.
## PLAQUE OF OBA OZOLUA WITH WARRIORS AND ATTENDANTS

Edo
Benin Kingdom, Nigeria
16th/17th century
Brass; 38.5 x 39 x 2 cm (15 ⅛ x 15 ⅜ x ³⁄₁₆ in.)
Museum für Völkerkunde Wien, 64.717

Oba Ozolua, at center, is depicted wearing a garment of overlapping leaf-shaped plates, possibly his famous protective coat of iron. Snakes, which Olokun, the god of the waters, sent to guard the divine leader, run down the garment's torso and arms. In his right hand, Ozolua holds an eben sword, a symbol of leadership. His other hand grasps a spear that is also held by his trusted friend Laisolobi, who ultimately betrayed him in order to free his exhausted soldiers. This story teaches that the abuse of power can be the downfall of even the strongest, most influential leaders.

9.
## EWUA OFFICIAL

Edo
Benin Kingdom, Nigeria
18th century (?)
Brass; 62 x 20 x 17 cm (24 ⅜ x 7 ⅞ x 6 ¹⁄₁₆ in.)
The Trustees of the National Museums of Scotland,
Edinburgh, A 1985.631

This figure wears a beautifully patterned tunic and wrapper and a cross-shaped pendant low on his chest. In his right hand, he carries a brass-caster's hammer—a tool used by smiths to manipulate red-hot metal—which symbolizes both the creative force and also Ogun, the god of iron and warfare. The man may be an ewua official, whose tasks include awakening the oba at dawn with rituals honoring his dynasty and its origins, a practice initiated by Oba Esigie in the sixteenth century. Ewua officials are often portrayed wearing a cross, a sign that predates the Portuguese arrival in Benin, though its meaning was enhanced by its similarity to the cross of the Portuguese Order of Christ.

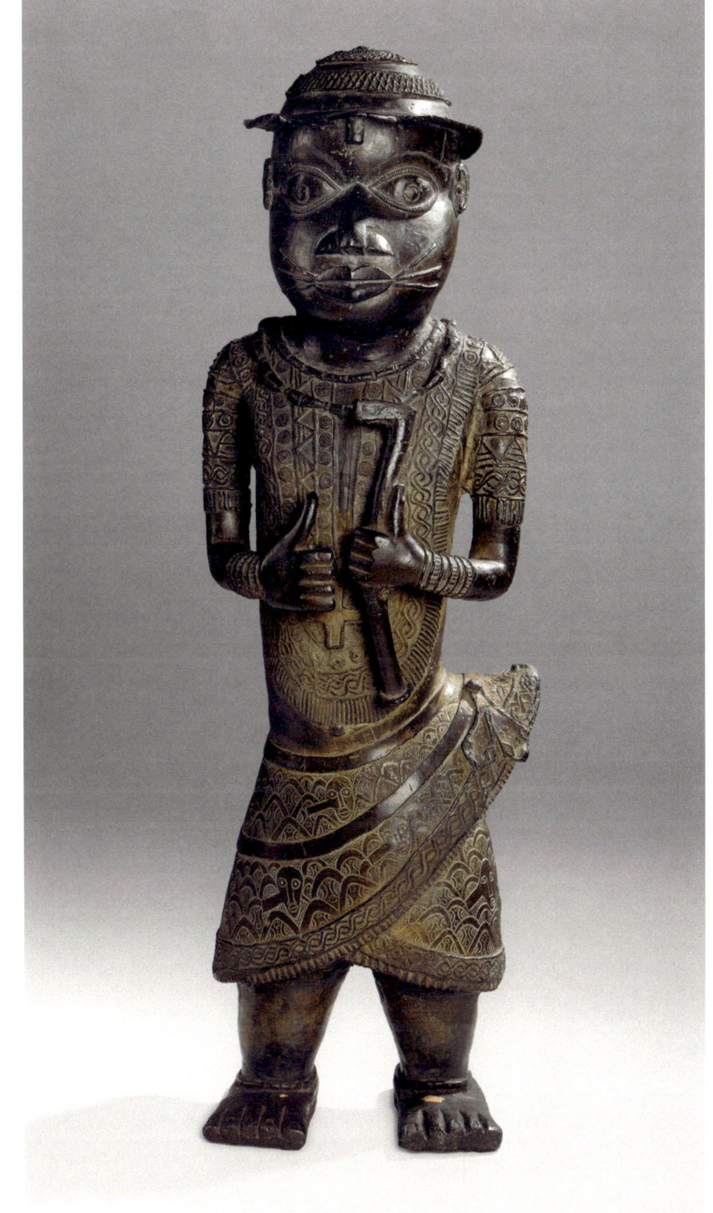

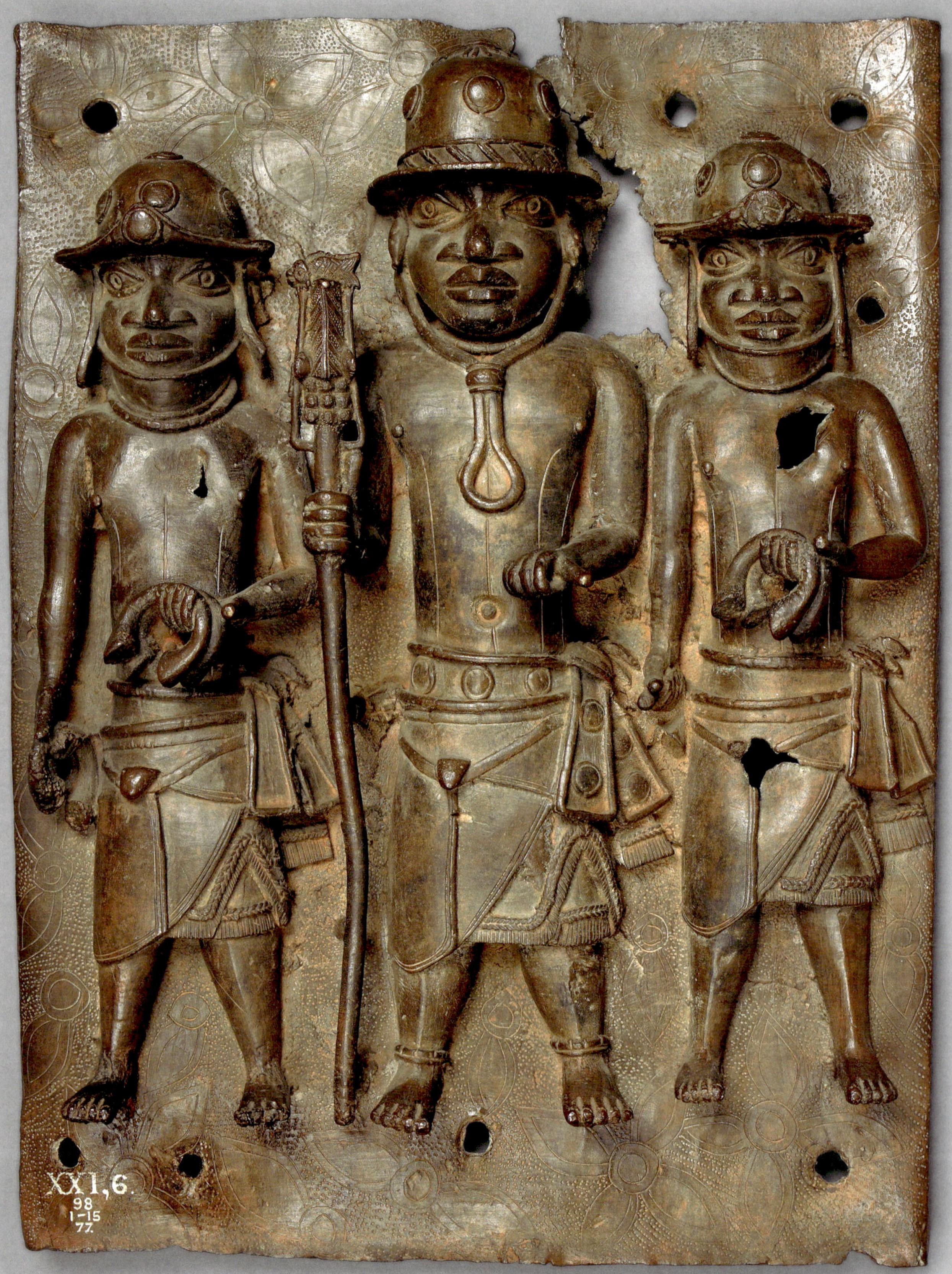

10.
## PLAQUE OF THREE TRADERS FROM BENIN

Edo
Benin Kingdom, Nigeria
16th/17th century
Brass; 48.5 x 37 x 9 cm (19 ⅛ x 14 ⅝ x 3 ⁹⁄₁₆ in.)
The Trustees of the British Museum, London,
Af1898, 0115.77

The helmets worn by these men and the staff held
by the central figure, which is surmounted by the
head of a crocodile biting a fish, are emblems of
the royal guild of traders. Fittingly, the crocodile,
an animal that inhabits both water and land,
is associated with the Portuguese, who likewise
traversed both terrains. Crocodiles also represent
Olokun, the god of the waters and the wealth they
deliver. The two flanking figures hold manillas,
brass rings that were an important form of
currency along Africa's west coast.

11.
## SALTCELLAR

Edo
Benin Kingdom, Nigeria
Early 16th century
Ivory; 19.2 x 7.2 x 8 cm (7 ⁹⁄₁₆ x 2 ⅞ x 3 ³⁄₁₆ in.)
Ethnographic Museum Antwerp, AE 1974.25.1
(1–4)

Members of Benin's royal guild of ivory carvers
began making elaborate curios for Portuguese
travelers not long after the establishment of
coastal trade. Among the most popular items were
spoons, forks, hunting horns, and saltcellars, such
as this two-chambered example. The expert carver
who created this work is known for his depictions
of Portuguese horsemen; the horse on the lid
probably also once carried a rider. In the sixteenth
century, salt was a valuable commodity that only
the wealthiest Europeans could afford.

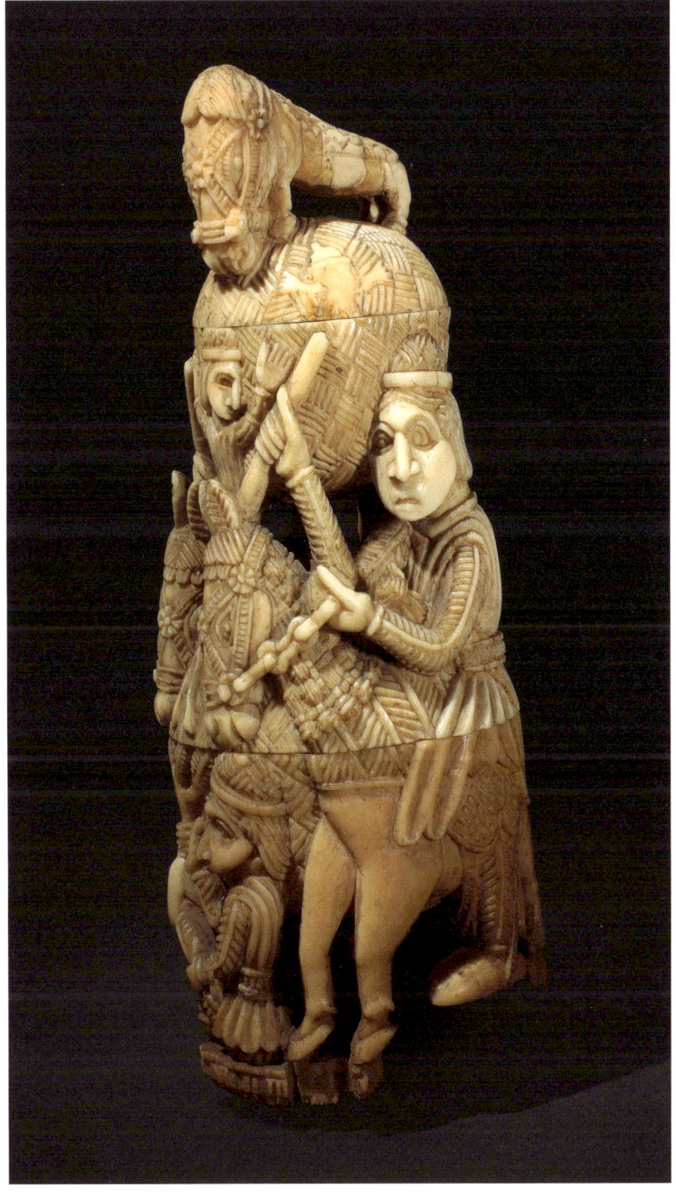

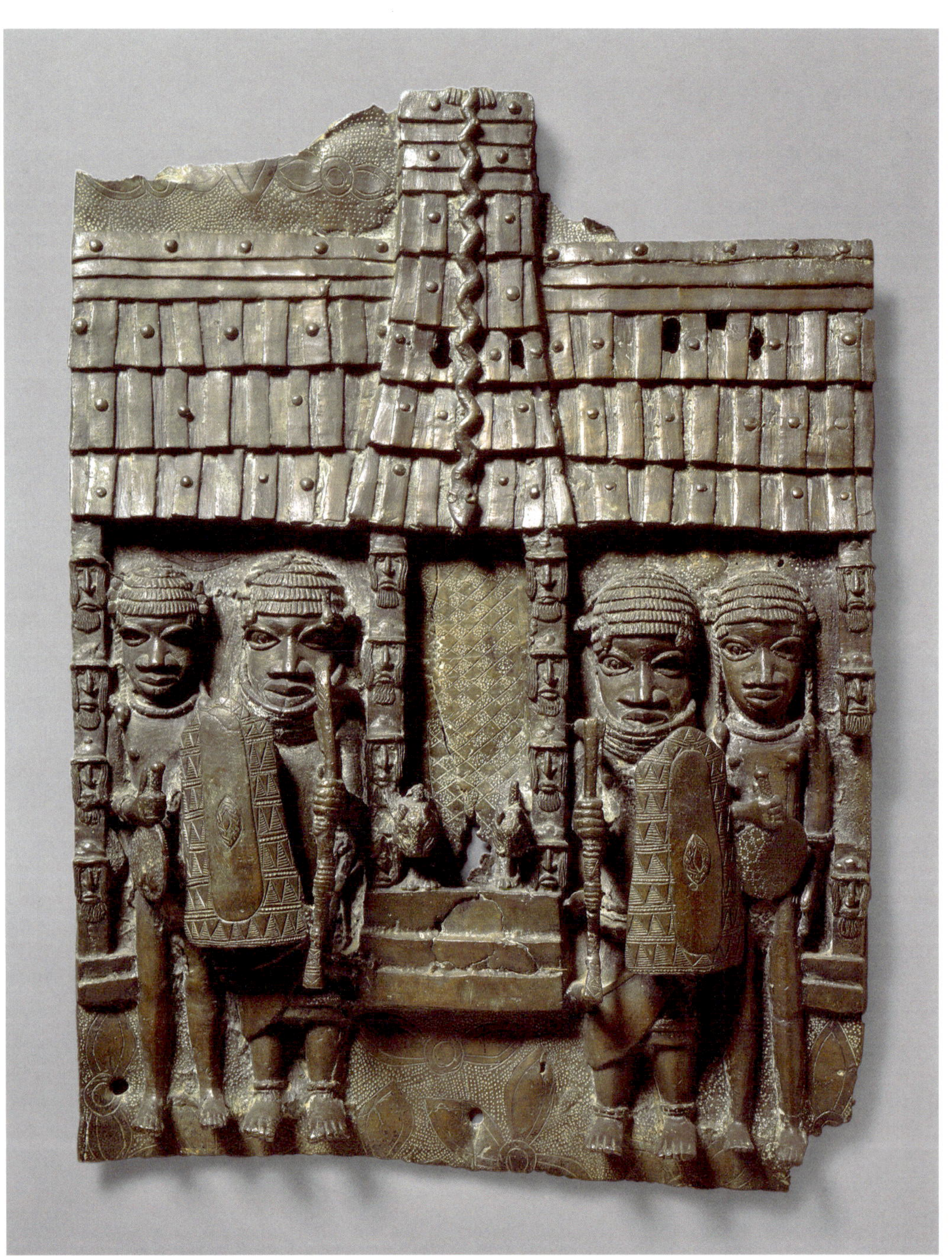

12.

## PLAQUE OF A PALACE INTERIOR

Edo
Benin Kingdom, Nigeria
16th/17th century
Brass; 52 x 40 cm (20 ½ x 15 ¾ in.)
Staatliche Museen zu Berlin,
Ethnologisches Museum, III C 8377

This plaque beautifully illustrates
details of the oba's palace, including its
wood shingles attached with nails; the
brass snake, cast in sections, running
down its turret; and the pillars lined
with brass plaques here depicted
as Portuguese faces. The scene may
represent a gate of entry or a passage
between inner courtyards. Turrets
are known to have marked such
transitional points within the large
palace complex. However, the pair
of leopards (now damaged) standing
on either side of the doorway may
indicate that it is the entrance to a
royal altar.

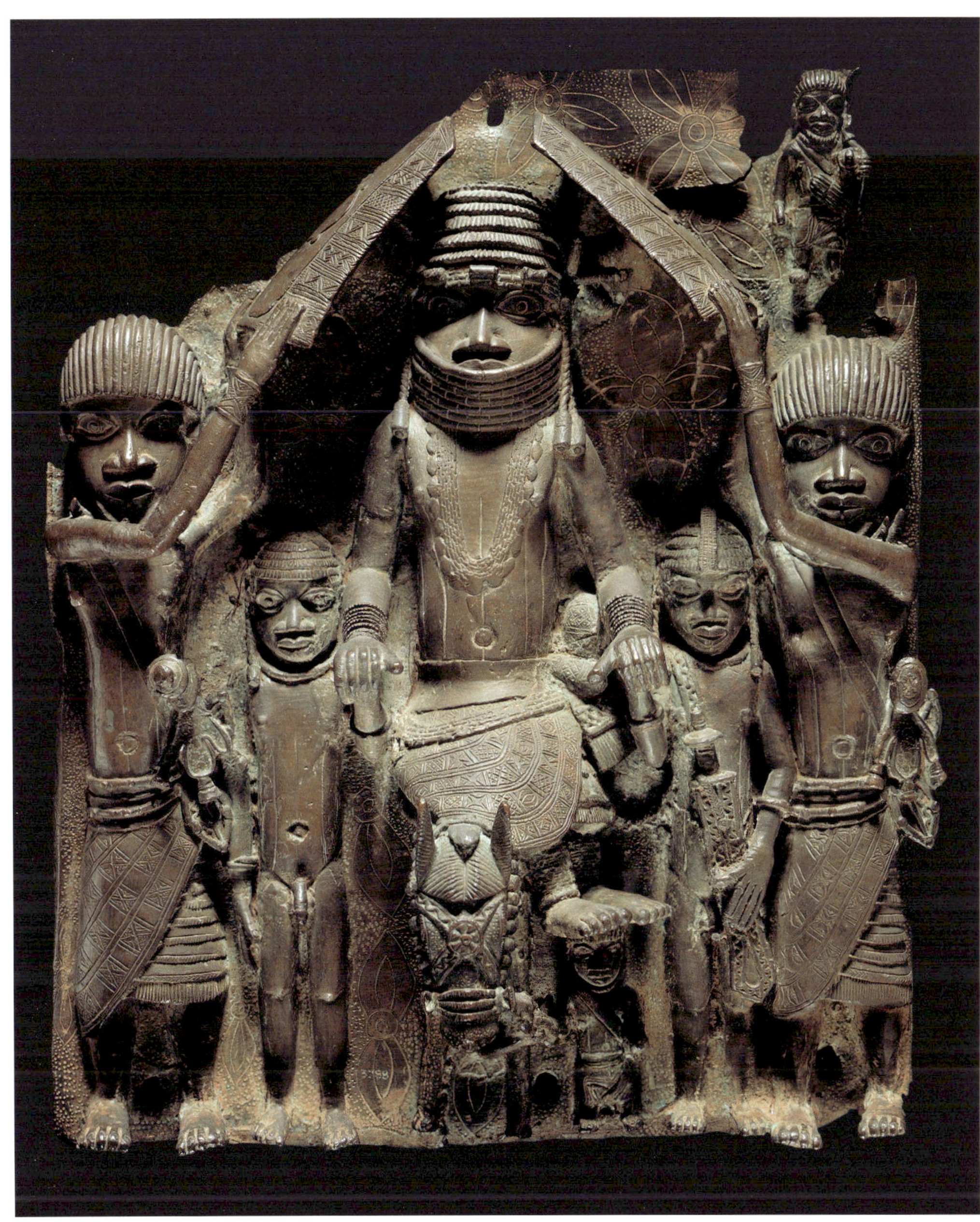

13.

**PLAQUE OF OBA ESIGIE ON HORSEBACK WITH ATTENDANTS**
Edo
Benin Kingdom, Nigeria
16th/17th century
Brass; 48 x 39 cm (18 ⅞ x 15 ⅜ in.)
Staatliche Museen zu Berlin,
Ethnologisches Museum, III C 8056

During the sixteenth and seventeenth centuries, the oba and the highest-ranking members of his court rode horses in warfare and during ritual processions. Here, an oba is portrayed riding sidesaddle in a stately procession accompanied by youthful servants supporting his arms and higher-ranking officials shielding his head. The oba is almost certainly Esigie, who is called "the ruler on horseback."

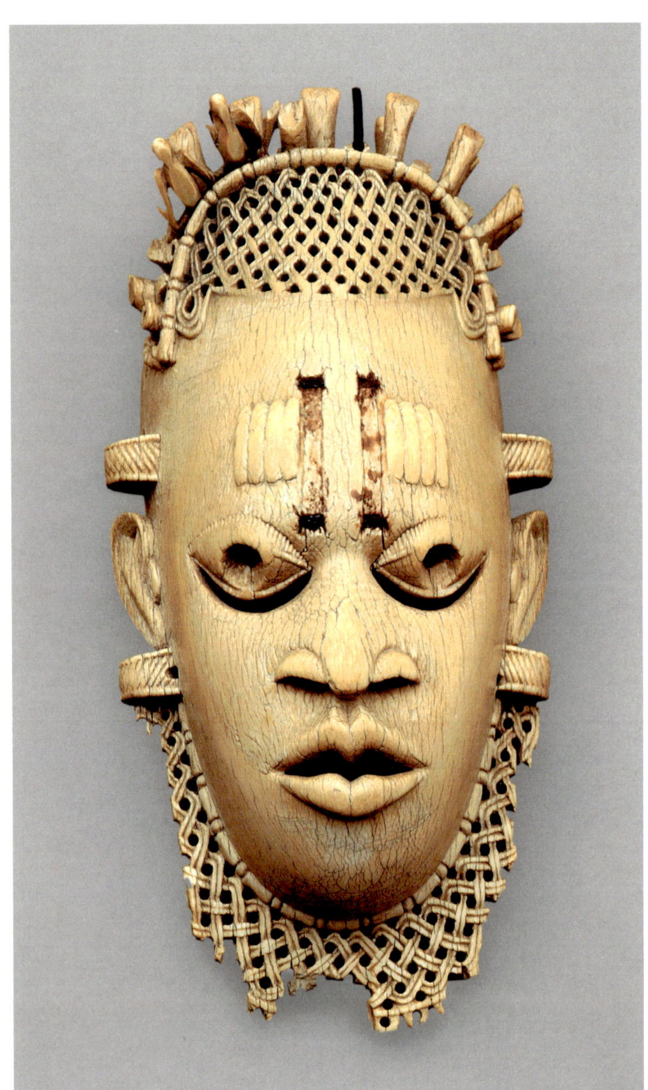

14.

**HIP PENDANT OF IYOBA IDIA**
Edo
Benin Kingdom, Nigeria
Early/mid-16th century
Ivory and iron; 12 x 6.5 cm (4 ¾ x 2 ⁹⁄₁₆ in.)
Seattle Art Museum, gift of Katherine White and
the Boeing Company, 81.17.493

This extraordinary object is one of a group of
four ivory hip pendants depicting Iyoba Idia,
which are among Benin's most iconic artworks.
Each pendant features a sensitively rendered
face with iron inserts at the eyelids and brow
that express a determined demeanor. The use of
ivory underscores the value and sacredness of the
pendants and their close association to the oba.
Today, the oba wears a contemporary version of
the iyoba pendant as part of his ritual attire at
Igue, the annual series of rites that cleanse and
purify the kingdom, reaffirm its hierarchy, and
reinvigorate the oba's spiritual potency.

15.

**ALTAR GROUP (*ASEBERIA*) WITH AN IYOBA
AND ATTENDANTS**
Edo
Benin Kingdom, Nigeria
17th/18th century
Brass; 33 x 30.5 x 23.5 cm (13 x 12 x 9 ¼ in.)
The Trustees of the National Museums of Scotland,
Edinburgh, A 1898.380

In Benin the practice of creating figural groupings
for royal altars dates to the seventeenth century.
This work was made for an iyoba's altar and shows
her at the center, wearing a coral-beaded cap over
her distinguishing "chicken's beak" hairstyle.
Flanking her are female attendants who hold
aloft mirrored charms that act as gateways into
the otherworld. Warriors and ewua officials, each
important members of her court, are also in the
procession. Two leopards (see cat. 20), symbols of
the oba's power, stand at the front.

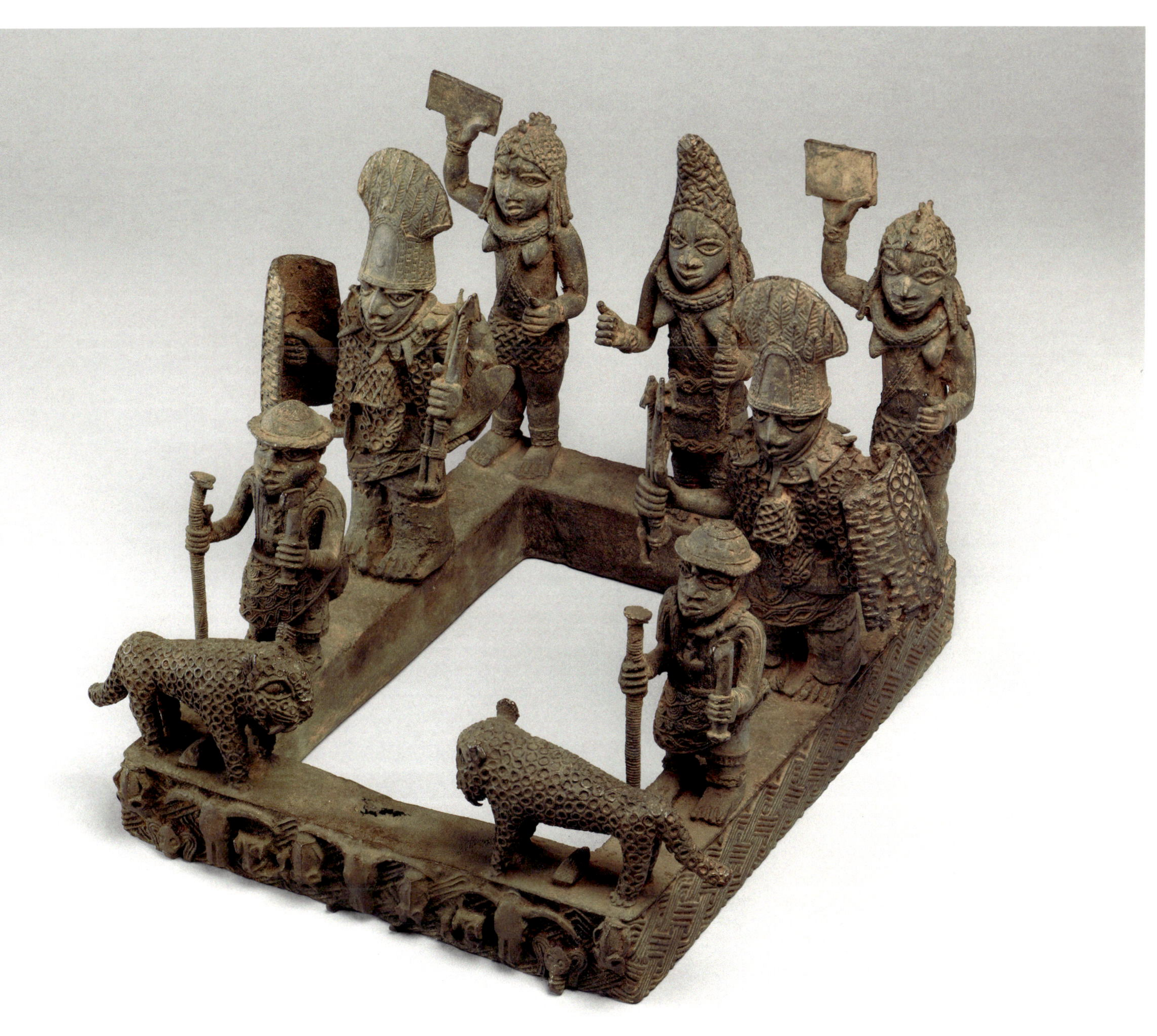

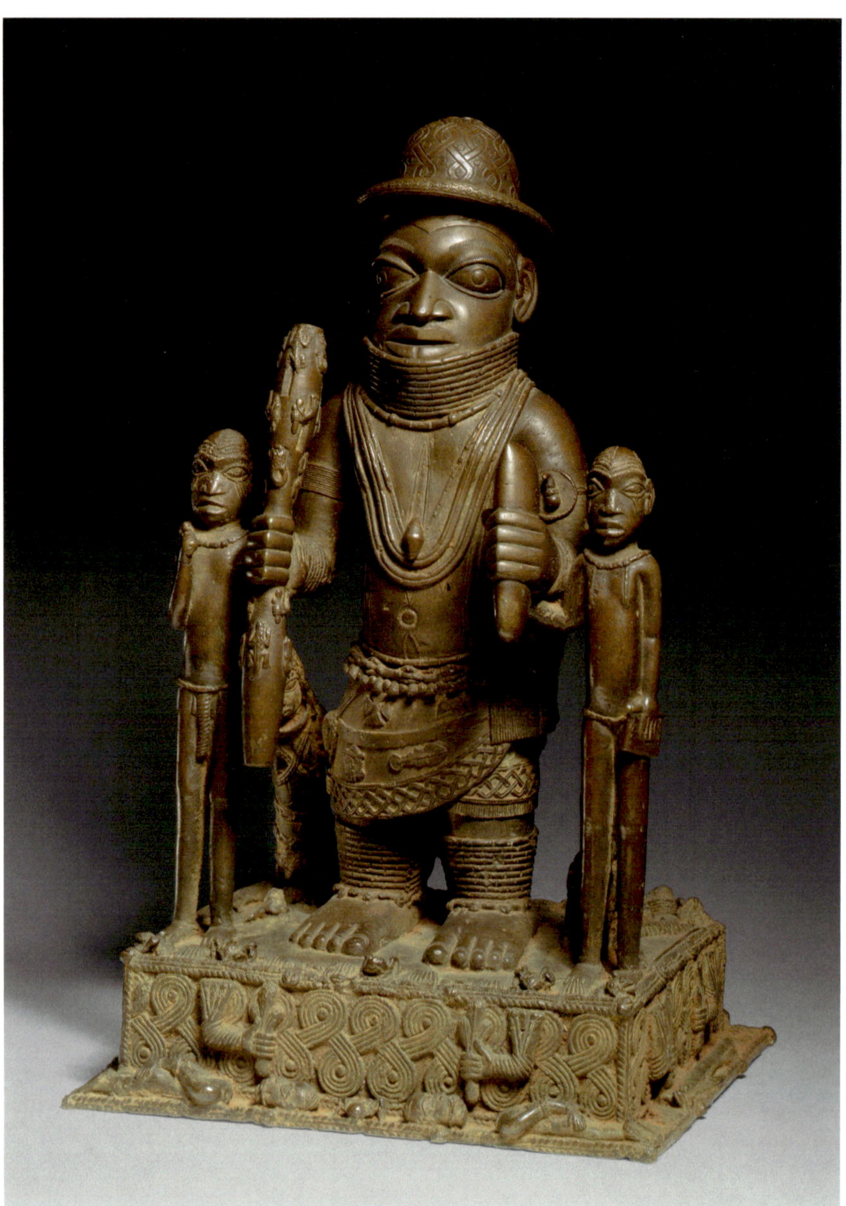

16.

## ALTAR GROUP (*ASEBERIA*) WITH OBA EWUAKPE AND ATTENDANTS

Edo
Benin Kingdom, Nigeria
18th century
Brass; h.: 58 cm (22 ⅞ in.)
Staatliche Museen zu Berlin, Ethnologisches
Museum, III C 8165

Oba Ewuakpe is a pivotal figure in the history of the Benin Kingdom. After being driven from the throne in a rebellion, he worked his way back to power by means of worldly diplomacy and otherworldly intervention. Here, he is depicted at one of his lowest points, stripped of the bulk of his coral regalia and assisted by slaves rather than members of his court. However, he still wears the power-invested stone bead (ivie egbo) at his chest, proof that he is the oba by right.

17.

## ALTAR GROUP (*ASEBERIA*) WITH OBA AKENZUA I AND ATTENDANTS

Edo
Benin Kingdom, Nigeria
18th century
Brass; h.: 63 cm (24 ¾ in.)
Staatliche Museen zu Berlin, Ethnologisches
Museum, III C 8164

This work honors Oba Akenzua I and probably stood on an altar dedicated to him. Altar groups were an innovation of the seventeenth century, and their style—bulky, hierarchical, and crowded with imagery—is indicative of the complicated political intrigues of the day. In his right hand, Akenzua holds a staff commemorating his victory over Iyase n'Ode, a supporter of Akenzua's brother, who tried to overthrow him.

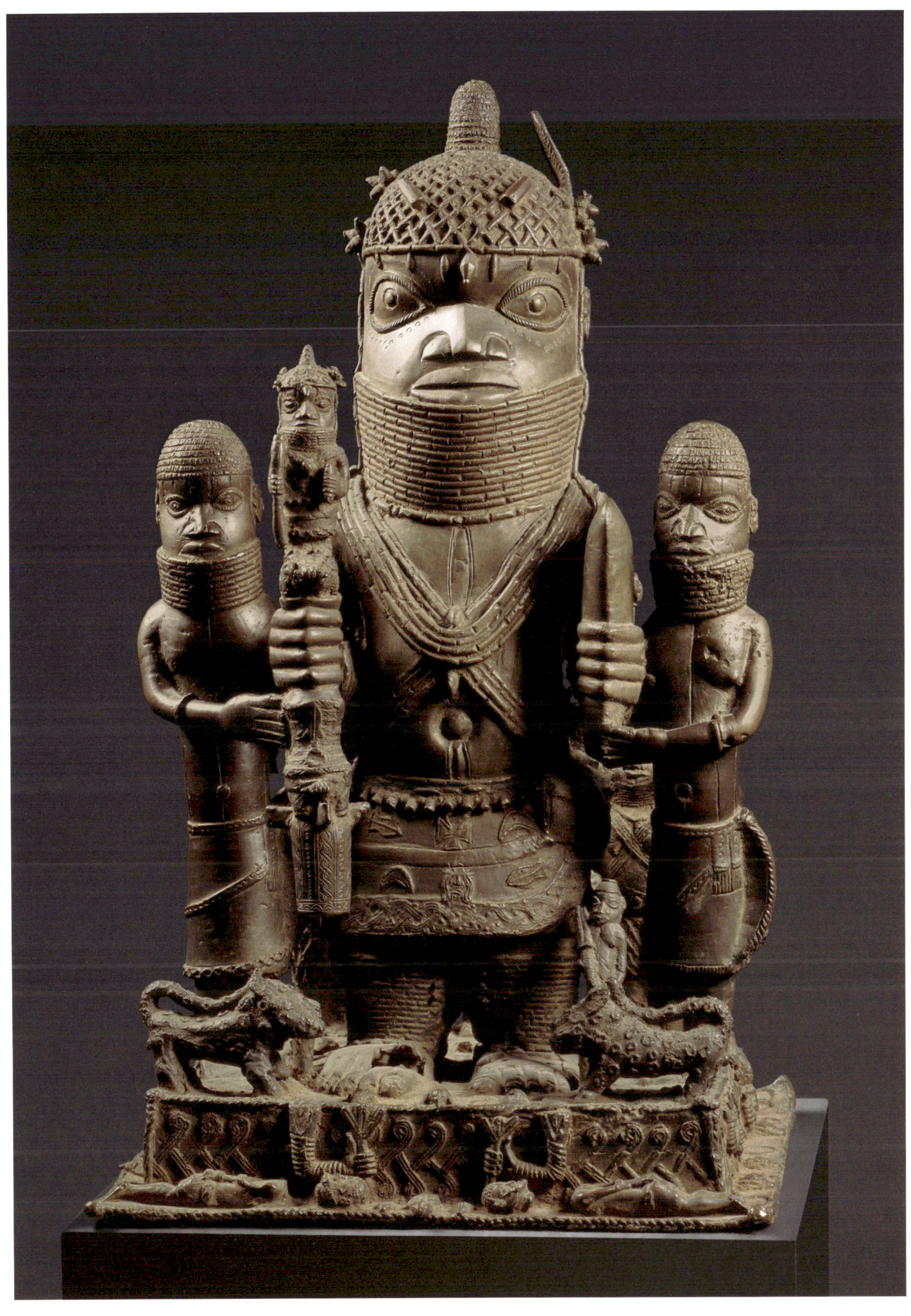

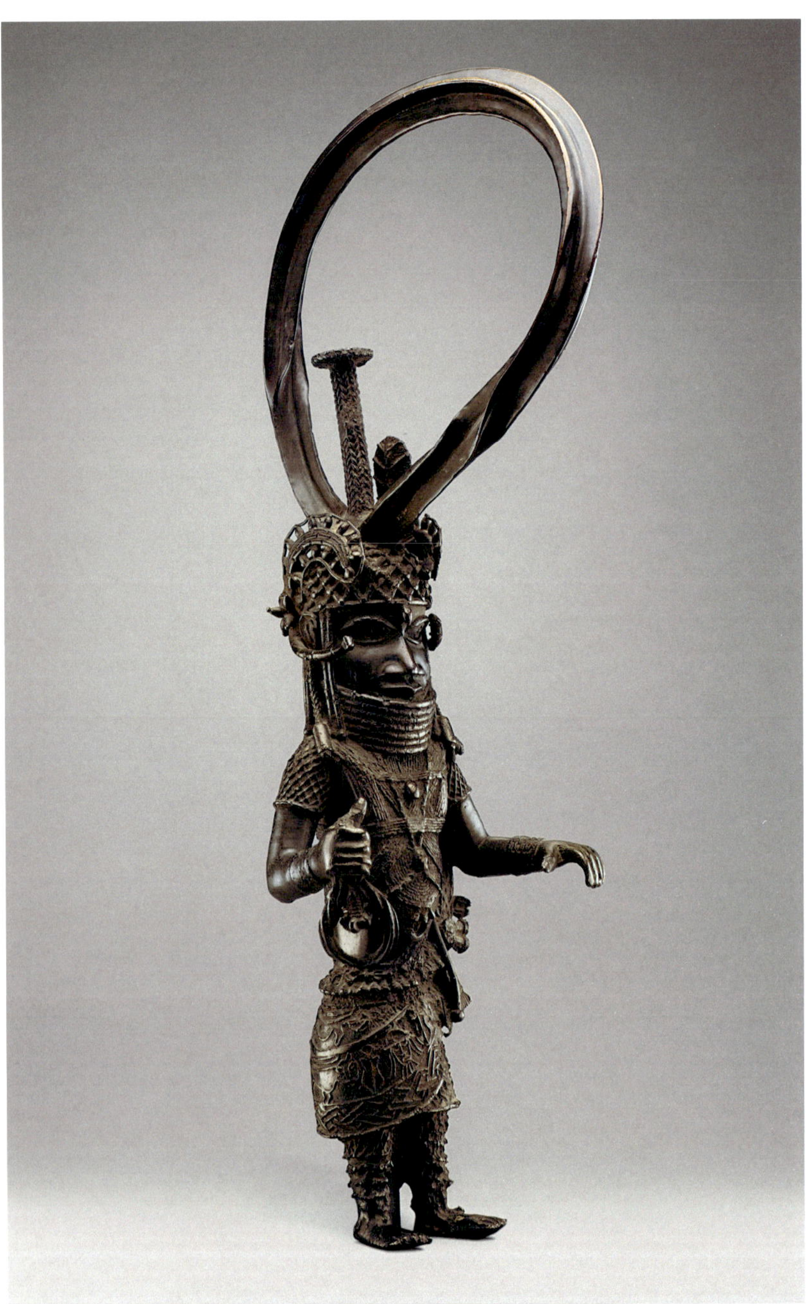

18.

### ALTAR FIGURE OF AN OBA

Edo
Benin Kingdom, Nigeria
17th/18th century
Brass; h.: 53.5 cm (21 in.)
Private collection

This figure was made for an oba's ancestral altar. The rod extending through it, which is encircled by a protective ring, connected it more fully to the world beyond. The figure holds an eben sword (now broken) in his right hand; his other hand suggests the patting gesture the oba employs at Emobo, the final rite of the Igue festival that reinvigorates his spiritual powers. The motion calmly but firmly pushes unsettled spirits from the kingdom. Here, the movement probably prevented intrusive supernatural forces from stealing the sustenance that the altar provided for the oba's deified ancestors.

19.

### PAIR OF ARM CUFFS

Edo
Benin Kingdom, Nigeria
18th century
Ivory; left: 13 x 9 cm (5 ⅛ x 3 9/16 in.)
right: 13.1 x 9.1 cm (5 3/16 x 3 9/16 in.)
The Trustees of the British Museum, London, Af1922, 0313.5–6

An extraordinary eighteenth-century carver made these finely detailed ivory arm cuffs. On two sides of each cuff, the oba holds a raised eben sword and is accompanied by helmeted warriors, stressing his control of Benin's military might. This imagery alternates with another group of figures (illustrated here) that centers on a high-ranking individual— possibly the ezomo, Benin's top war chief, who may have commissioned these cuffs. He is richly dressed and also holds a raised eben sword. Portuguese soldiers flank him, a reference to their role as Benin's military allies in the sixteenth century.

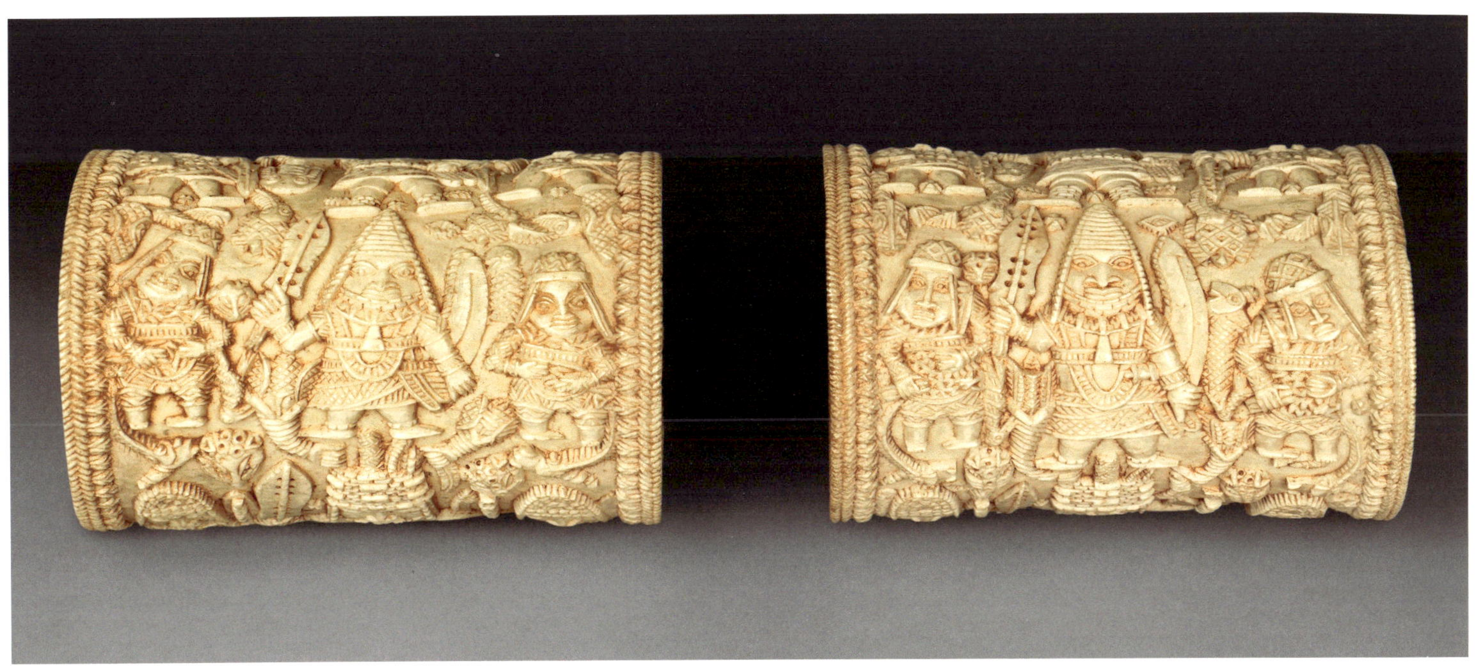

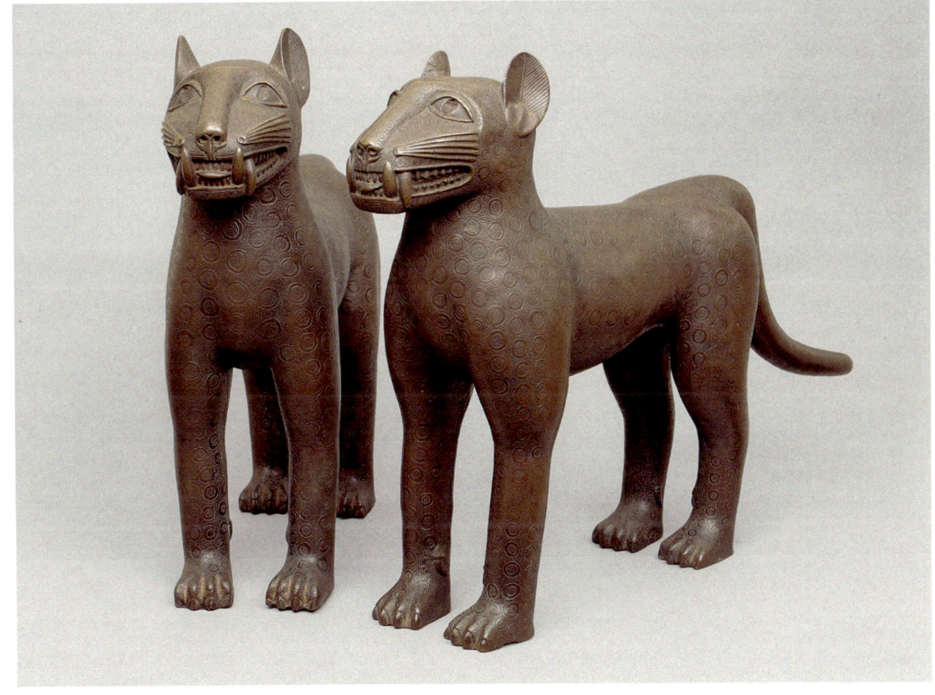

20.

## PAIR OF LEOPARDS
Edo
Benin Kingdom, Nigeria
16th/18th century
Brass; left: 50 x 79 x 15 cm (19 ⅝ x 31 ⅛ x 5 ⁵⁄₁₆ in.)
right: 49 x 77 x 14 cm (19 ¼ x 30 ⅜ x 5 ½ in.)
The National Commission for Museums and
Monuments, Nigeria, 52.13.1–2

Leopards are among the most emblematic
symbols of the oba. They are considered his
kingly counterpart in the wilderness and
are respected for their beauty, intelligence,
and predatory skills. Emphasizing this
correspondence, when an oba dies it is said that
"the leopard has returned to his lair." Prior to the
twentieth century, the oba kept domesticated
leopards in the palace to demonstrate mastery
over an opposing realm. This exquisite pair may
have stood on the altar of a deceased oba or
may have been placed on either side of the oba's
throne. In Benin, such ritual pairing evokes the
importance of spiritual balance.

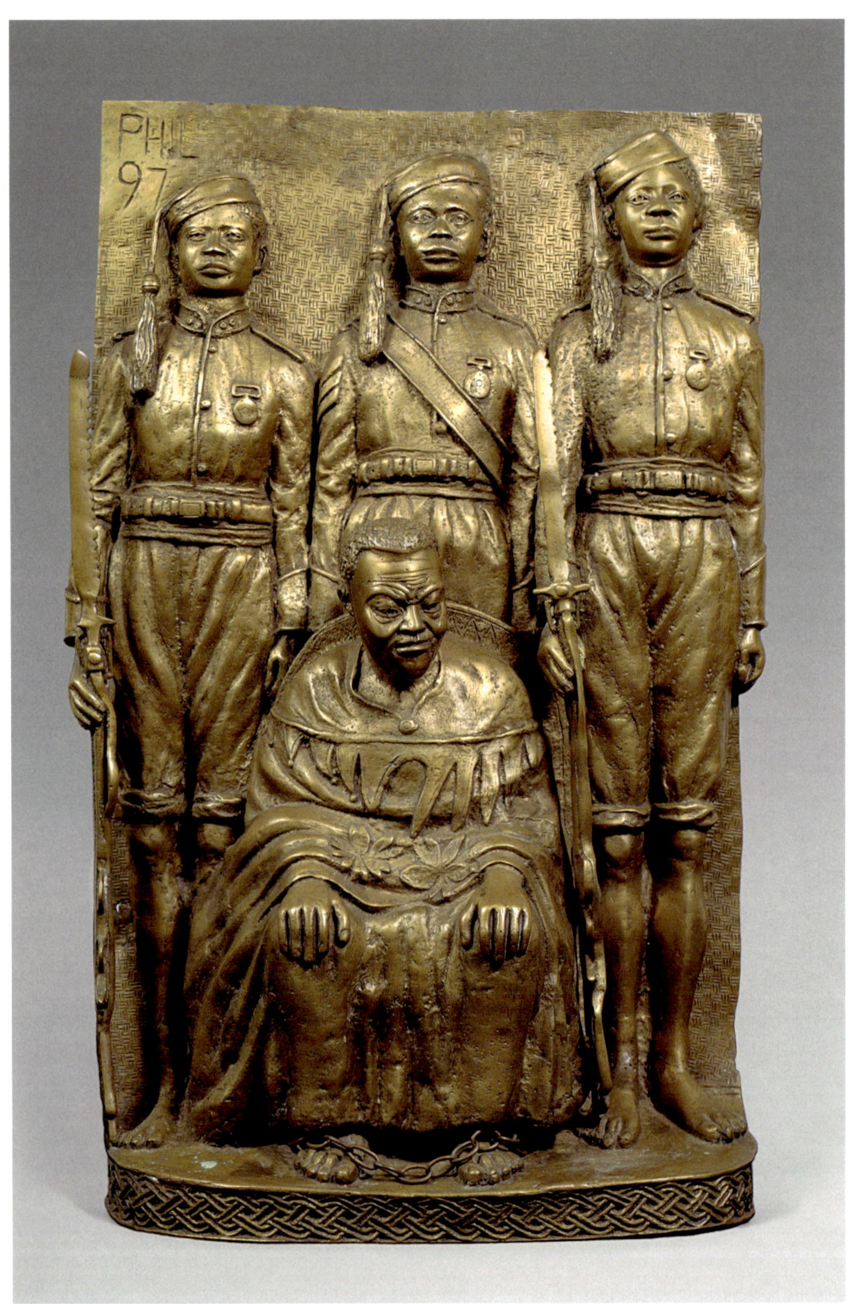



21.

## PLAQUE OF OBA OVONRAMWEN
## ON HIS WAY TO EXILE

Philip Omodamwen (active late 20th century)
Benin City, Nigeria
1997
Brass; 62.5 x 29 x 14 cm (24 ⅝ x 11 ⁷⁄₁₆ x 5 ½ in.)
Collection of High Priest Osemwegie Ebohon,
Benin City

Since 1997, the centennial of the British
Punitive Expedition to Benin, the exile of Oba
Ovonramwen has become a popular theme in
Benin's royal arts. This plaque is based on a
historic photograph (see fig. 10, p. 12) that shows
Ovonramwen aboard the British steam yacht *Ivy*
on his way to exile in Calabar. Philip Omodamwen
faithfully depicted the oba's velvet robe and trio
of guards, while accentuating the oba's shackles,
strained expression, and forward leaning pose,
which adds a heightened sense of tragic loss.

22.

## BOAT COMPOSITION

Omodamwen workshop
Benin City, Nigeria
2006
Brass; 44 x 126 x 35 cm (17 ⅜ x 49 ⅝ x 13 ¾ in.)
Museum für Völkerkunde Wien, 185.018

This contemporary depiction of Oba
Ovonramwen's journey into exile recasts and
embellishes the historic event. In contrast
to contemporaneous photographs showing
Ovonramwen on the British yacht *Ivy*, here he is
depicted heroically in full coral regalia and seated
at the center of a large canoe, accompanied by
a chief, two wives, four British soldiers, and two
rowers. For many Edo, the defeat and exile of
Ovonramwen continues to be a sacrilegious topic
that is not openly discussed.

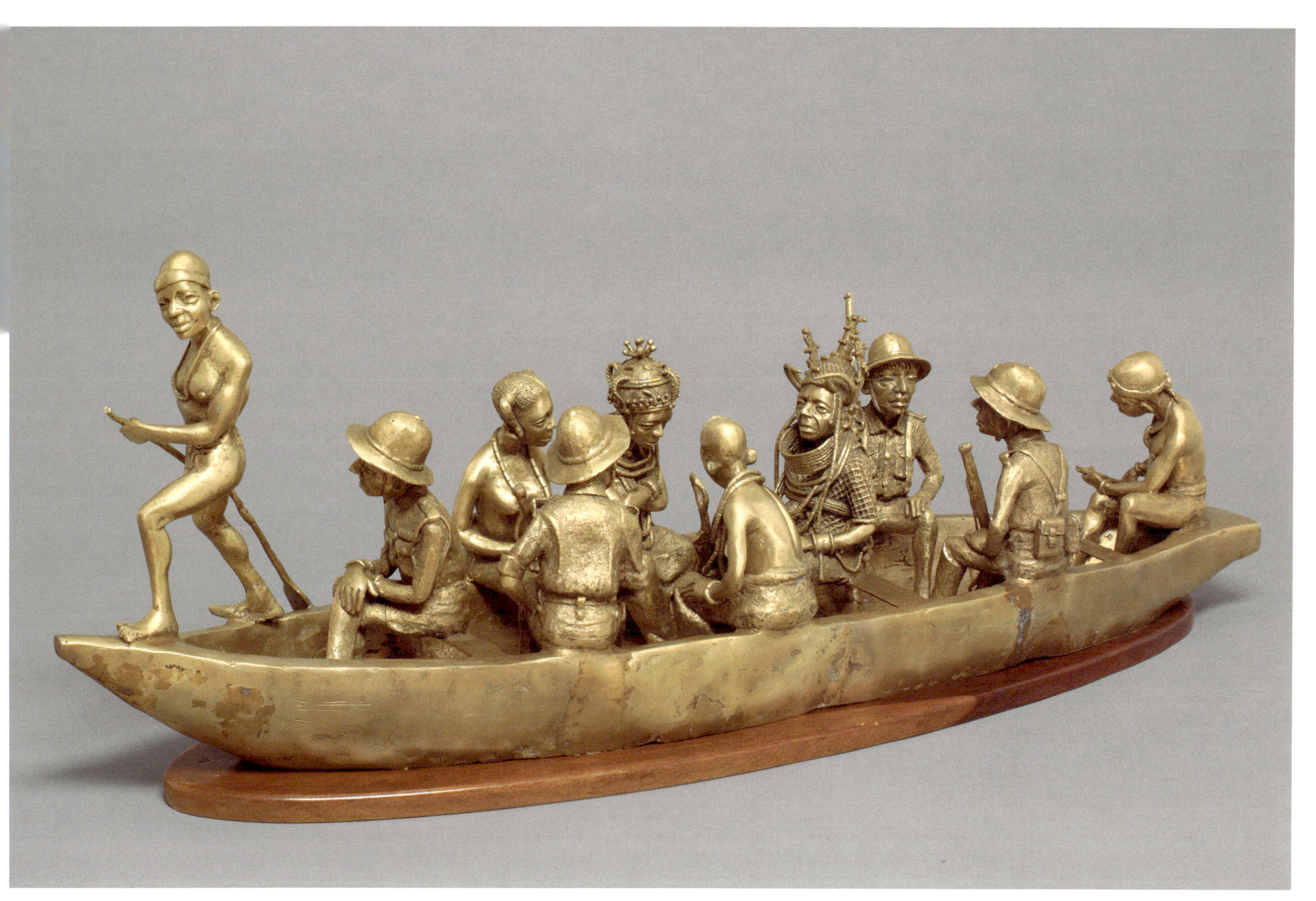

## BIBLIOGRAPHY

Ben-Amos, Paula. 1983. "In Honor of Queenmothers." In Paula Ben-Amos and Arnold Rubin, editors, *The Art of Power, the Power of Art: Studies in Benin Iconography*. Museum of Cultural History, UCLA, monograph series 19, pp. 79–83.

Ben-Amos, Paula Girshick. 1995. *The Art of Benin*. Revised edition. Smithsonian Institution Press.

———. 1999. *Art, Innovation and Politics in Eighteenth-Century Benin*. Indiana University Press.

Ben-Amos Girshick, Paula. 2007a. "Altar Group—*aseberia*—with Oba Akenzua I." In Plankensteiner 2007a, p. 472.

———. 2007b. "Altar Group—*aseberia*—with Oba Ewuakpe." In Plankensteiner 2007a, pp. 470–72.

Blackmun, Barbara W. 1990. "Oba's Portraits in Benin." *African Arts* 23, 3 (July), pp. 61–69, 102–04.

———. 1991. "Who Commissioned the Queen Mother Tusks? A Problem in the Chronology of Benin Ivories." *African Arts* 24, 2 (April), pp. 54–65, 90–91.

———. 2007a. "Pair of Armcuffs." In Plankensteiner 2007a, p. 352.

———. 2007b. "Relief Plaque: Oba Esigie on Horseback with Retainers." In Plankensteiner 2007a, pp. 441–42.

———. 2007c. "Who are the Figures in Benin Art? Translations from Ivory to Bronze." In Plankensteiner 2007a, pp. 161–69.

Bradbury, R. E. 1973. *Benin Studies*. Edited by Peter Morton-Williams. Oxford University Press.

Coombes, Annie E. 1994. *Reinventing Africa: Museums, Material Culture and Popular Imagination*. Yale University Press.

Curnow, Kathy. 1997. "The Art of Fasting: Benin's Auge Ceremony." *African Arts* 30, 4 (Autumn), pp. 46–53, 93–94.

Egharevba, Jacob U. 1968. *A Short History of Benin*. 1936. 4th edition. Ibadan University Press.

Eweka, Prince E. B. 1992. *Evolution of Benin Chieftaincy Titles*. Uniben Press.

Gallagher, Jackie. 1983. "'Fetish Belong King': Fish in the Art Benin." In Paula Ben-Amos and Arnold Rubin, editors, *The Art of Power, the Power of Art: Studies in Benin Iconography*. Museum of Cultural History, UCLA, monograph series 19, pp. 89–93.

Gore, Charles. 1997. "Casting Identities in Contemporary Benin." *African Arts* 30, 3 (Summer), pp. 54–61, 93.

Home, Robert. 1982. *City of Blood Revisited: A New Look at the Benin Expedition of 1897*. Rex Collings.

Igbafe, Philip Aigbana. 1970a. "The Changing Status of the Oba of Benin under Colonial Rule since Independence." In Michael Crowder and Obaro Ikime, editors, *West African Chiefs: Their Changing Status under Colonial Rule and Independence*. Africana Publishing Company.

———. 1970b. "The Fall of Benin: A Reassessment." *The Journal of African History* 11, 3, pp. 385–400.

———. 2007. "A History of the Benin Kingdom: an Overview." In Plankensteiner 2007a, pp. 41–54.

Inneh, Daniel. 2007. "The Guilds Working for the Palace." In Plankensteiner 2007a, pp. 103–18.

Jones, Adam. 1998. *Olfert Dapper's Description of Benin, 1668*. African Studies Program, University of Wisconsin–Madison.

Kaplan, Flora Edouwaye S. 2007. "Women in Benin Society and Art." In Plankensteiner 2007a, pp. 141–50.

Layiwola, Adepeju. 2007. "The Benin-Massacre: Memories and Experiences." In Plankensteiner 2007a, pp. 83–89.

Luschan, Felix von. 1919. *Die Altertümer von Benin*. 3 volumes. Vereinigung wissenschaftlicher Verleger.

Nevadomsky, Joseph. 1986. "The Benin Bronze Horseman as the Ata of Idah." *African Arts* 19, 4 (August), pp. 40–47, 85.

———. 1997. "Contemporary Art and Artists in Benin." *African Arts* 30, 4 (Autumn), pp. 54–63, 94–95.

Nevadomsky, Joseph and Greg Airihenbuwa. 2007. "The Rituals of Kingship and Hierarchy in the Benin Kingdom." In Plankensteiner 2007a, pp. 119–29.

Nevadomsky, Joseph and Agbonifo Osemweri. 2007. "Benin Art in the Twentieth Century." In Plankensteiner 2007a, pp. 255–61.

Paudrat, Jean-Louis. 2007. "Historiographic Notes on the Presence of the Court Art of Benin in France and the United States between 1930 and 1945." In Plankensteiner 2007a, pp. 235–45.

Plankensteiner, Barbara, ed. 2007a. *Benin—Kings and Rituals: Court Arts from Nigeria*. Exh. cat. Kunsthistoriches Museum Vienna mit MVK und ÖTM/Snoeck.

———. 2007b. "Introduction." In Plankensteiner 2007a, pp. 21–39.

———. 2007c. "The 'Benin Affair' and its Consequences." In Plankensteiner 2007a, pp. 199–211.

Ryder, Alan. 1969. *Benin and the Europeans, 1485–1897*. Longmans.

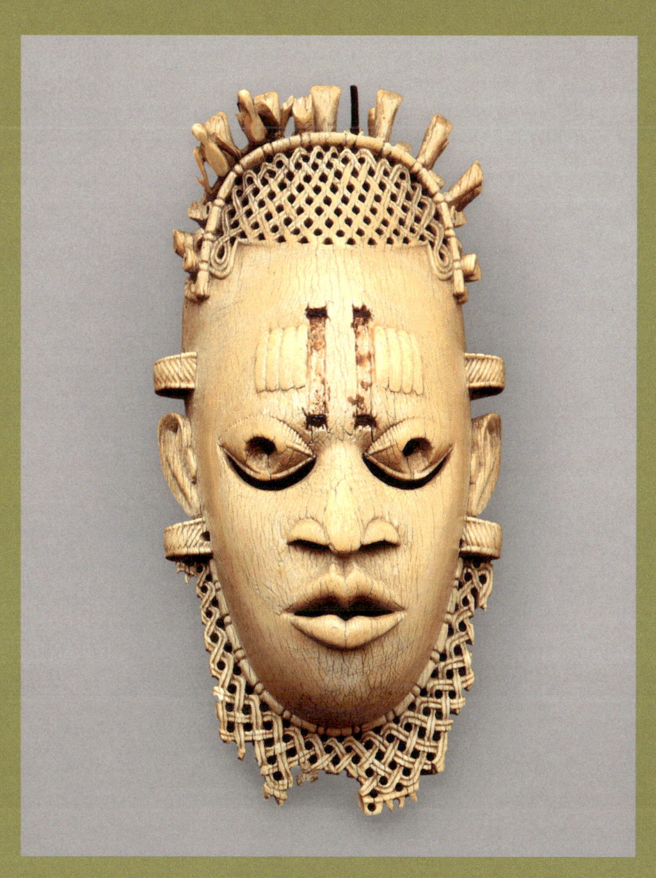

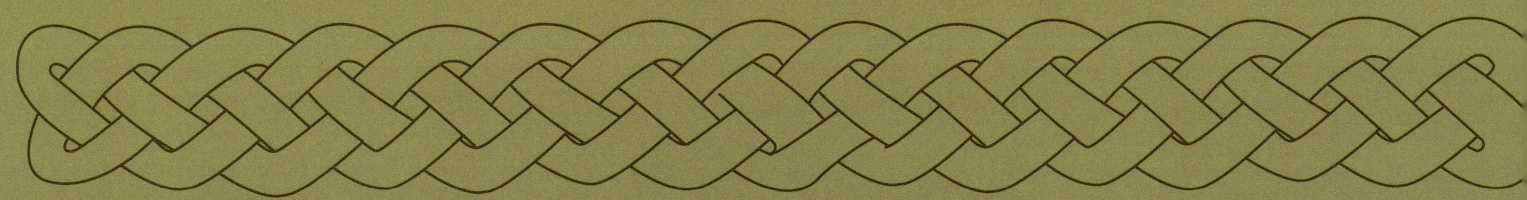

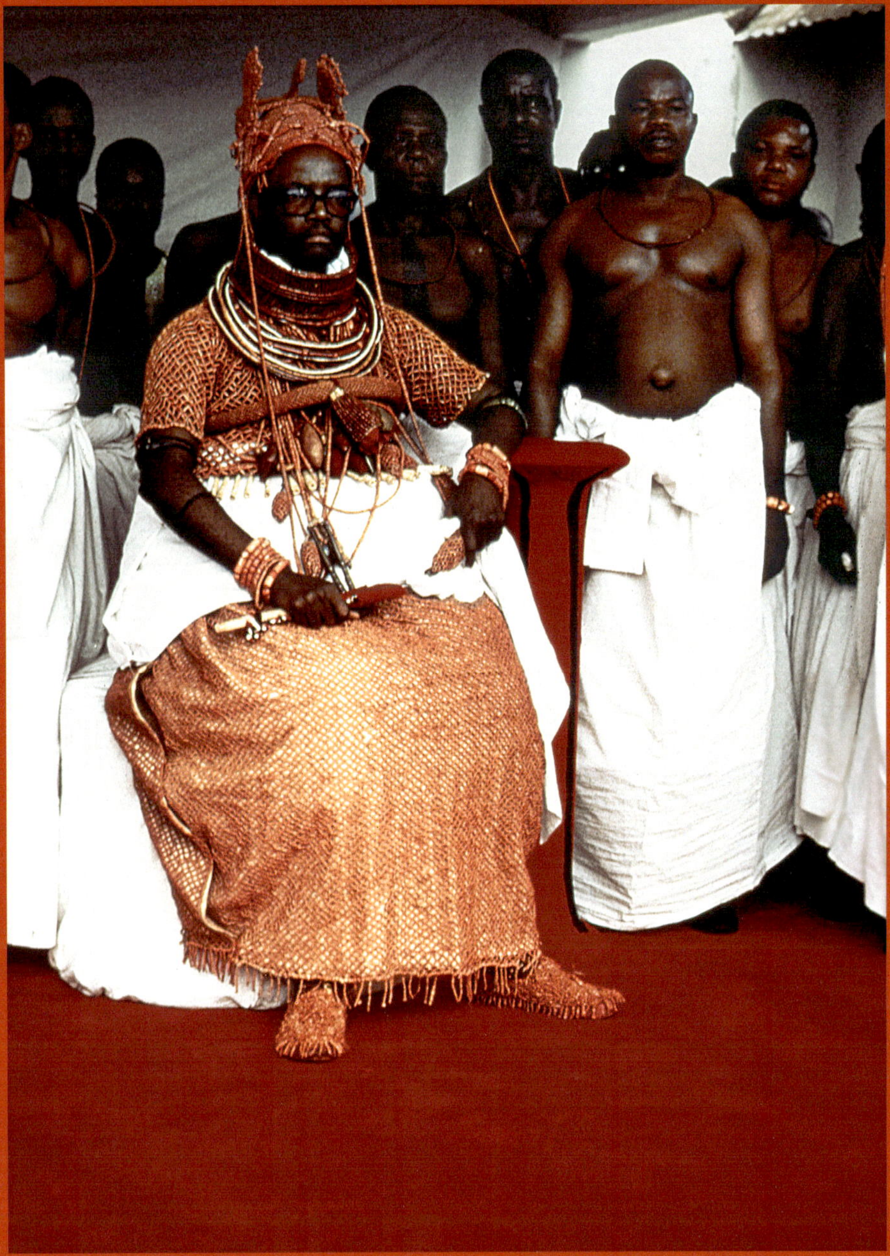

## BENIN: ROYAL ARTS OF A WEST AFRICAN KINGDOM

The Benin Kingdom, located in present-day southwestern Nigeria, has roots that stretch back to the thirteenth century. In the late fifteenth century, the kingdom established a mercantile relationship with Portugal, greatly increasing its wealth and might. Benin became a regional powerhouse and, under a long lineage of divine rulers, or obas, it wielded great economic and political influence. The obas also supported guilds of artists—chief among them brass casters and ivory carvers—whom they employed to produce objects that honor royal ancestors and glorify history and court life. The sophisticated creations of Benin's royal artists stand among the greatest works of African art today.

Published in concert with a major international exhibition, for which the Art Institute of Chicago is the sole North American venue, *Benin: Royal Arts of a West African Kingdom* highlights twenty-two masterworks that reveal the breadth and depth of the kingdom's artistic corpus, including finely cast brass figures, altar heads, and wall plaques, as well as ivory pendants, boxes, and arm cuffs embellished in detailed bas relief. An insightful essay by Art Institute curator Kathleen Bickford Berzock outlines the kingdom's history and sheds light on these works of art by describing their making and function in the context of the royal court.

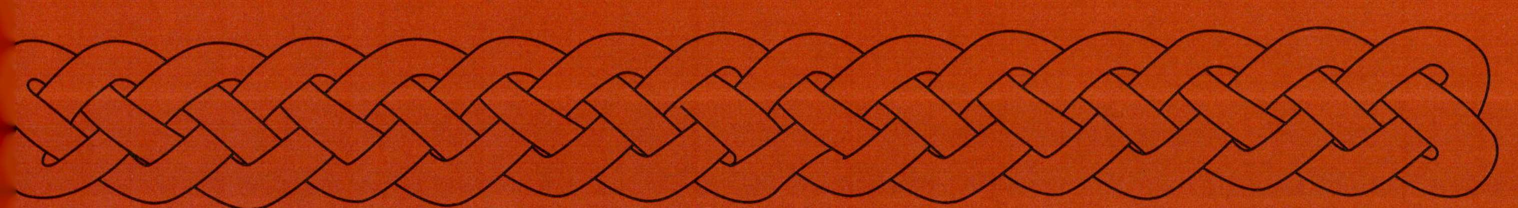